P9-DHT-602

ADAPTATION IN
CULTURAL EVOLUTION:
AN APPROACH TO
MEDICAL ANTHROPOLOGY

ADAPTATION IN
CULTURAL EVOLUTION

AN APPROACH TO
MEDICAL ANTHROPOLOGY

Alexander Alland, Jr.

Columbia University Press
New York and London

Alexander Alland is Associate Professor of Anthropology at Columbia University.

Chapter 3 is a greatly revised and expanded version of the article "Ecology and Adaptation to Parasitic Diseases," appearing in *Environment and Cultural Behavior,* edited by Andrew P. Vayda and published © 1969 by Natural History Press. It is reprinted with the permission of Doubleday and Company, Inc.

The major portion of Chapter 7 was first published as "Native Therapists and Western Medical Practitioners Among the Abron of the Ivory Coast" in *Transactions of the New York Academy of Sciences,* Ser. II, Vol. 26, No. 6 (April, 1964), pp. 714-25. Reprinted by permission.

Copyright © 1970 Columbia University Press
ISBN 0-231-03997-2
Library of Congress Catalog Card Number: 78-100666
Printed in the United States of America

10 9 8 7 6 5 4 3 2

To the memory of
V. Gordon Childe

PREFACE

My interest in human ecology, particularly its medical aspects, developed during my first field experience in the Ivory Coast, West Africa. There I was struck by the wide range of behaviors which made good sense in terms of basic hygiene. Among these were the use of pit latrines, apparently before European contact, frequent and thorough bathing, isolation of the sick in the case of certain highly contagious diseases, and the thorough cooking of food. The situation was, of course, by no means perfect, and many tropical diseases could be found in the population. Still, these people who had no concept of preventive medicine other than the use of charms to ward off disease had developed a basically sound set of hygiene practices. Furthermore, these practices contrasted with relatively ineffective therapeutic techniques which were solidly embedded in ethnomedical theory. In effect, the most successful behaviors from the medical point of view lay outside native medical practice as such.

These observations led me to examine the role of hygiene and therapy in relation to environmental adaptation. My thinking soon extended to ecological adjustments in general and their place in the evolution of human behavioral systems. The result is this book.

Thanks are due several individuals and organizations. My colleagues at Columbia University have provided a highly stimulating intellectual battleground. My work has been particularly influenced by Professors Marvin Harris, Andrew P. Vayda, and Robert F. Murphy. I owe a debt to Professor Paul Collins, who has sharpened all our ideas about functional systems.

Field research in Africa was supported by the Yale University Department of Anthropology and the Yale University Program in African Studies in the summer of 1960. Further field work in Africa was supported by a predoctoral grant from the National Institute of Mental Health of the United States Public Health Service, 1961-1962. Much of the research behind Chapter 4 was supported by a summer grant from the Columbia University Council for Research in the Social Sciences.

I also wish to thank the New York Academy of Sciences for permission to reprint my article "Native Therapists and Western Medical Practitioners Among the Abron of the Ivory Coast," which first appeared in the *Transactions of the New York Academy of Sciences*, Series II, Vol. 26, No. 6, April, 1964, pp. 714-25. This article forms the core of Chapter 7. Thanks go also to the Natural History Press for permission to reprint a revised and greatly expanded version of my paper "Ecology and Adaptation to Parasitic Diseases," which appeared in *Environment and Cultural Behavior*, edited by Andrew P. Vayda, 1969.

What follows in this book is offered as a tentative and somewhat speculative analysis of disease-oriented behavior in relation to human ecology and behavioral evolution. My hope is that this book will stimulate research of a comparative nature. It it only through such research that questions about adaptation to disease will finally be answered.

Alexander Alland, Jr.

CONTENTS

CHAPTER 1

INTRODUCTION

Anthropology has traditionally intruded upon other disciplines. It is perhaps the only scholarly pursuit which can be classified within the sciences, the social sciences, and the humanities. Recently a growing interest in human biocultural adaptation has led a number of anthropologists to consider data and theories derived from animal ecology, botany, geography, evolutionary biology, and cybernetics. While some scholars are able to master the material from one or two of these other disciplines, it is rarely possible to develop an expertise in all of them. In fact such an attempt is scarcely ever made. Instead the researcher concerned with "interdisciplinary" problems attempts to develop a working knowledge of the techniques and the literature in those fields which are crucial to his interests in research. This in turn increases his ability to ask meaningful questions which yield significant data open to cross disciplinary manipulation.

Up to the present time the major emphasis in

1

studies of biocultural adaptation has been upon economic exploitation. There is no doubt that subsistence patterns are among the most important cultural factors influencing ultimate population size. On the other hand, those aspects of culture which affect fertility, death, and disease rates are also major factors in the adaptation of human populations. The importance of disease goes beyond a simple mortality or fertility rate, for its presence provokes a wide variety of responses. Some of these responses, as we shall see later, reinforce social cohesion, while others are quite divisive. In many cases major areas of social structure are organized around what are essentially medical problems covering treatment, diagnosis, and preventive medicine.

In addition, economically productive behavior is frequently disjunctive with good health. Modern Western society is full of such examples, and there is no need to labor the point. It is in the study of technologically less advanced societies (where the number of variables is manageable) that these conflicts become particularly interesting for the student of adaptive systems. Such disjunctive situations present populations with game playing problems which must be solved reasonably well if the outcome of behavior is to be adaptive. The game involves the development of strategies (coordinated series of moves) which maximize gain and minimize loss for the population at large. Gain may result from increased output of energy either through the reduction of energy investment or through a change in the productive system which increases total output without an equivalent increase in investment. Loss may result from increased health hazards affecting fertility and/or mortality, and from a loss of total available input energy caused by various types of debilitating disease. The development of "good" minimax strategies improves population-environment relationships in terms of the number of individuals which a particular environment can support and is, therefore, in strictly biological terms, adaptive.

The game playing analogy can be extended to include interactions through time between specific populations and their environments (see Chapter 4). Because no environment is stable, populations must develop behavioral systems which tend to maximize adaptation to shifting conditions (see Davenport 1960). Particular aspects of behavior which may seem maladaptive from a synchronic point of view may in fact prove to be adaptive when put in a diachronic perspective. Such a game involves a population as one player and the environment as the other. One aspect of the environment's strategy involves periodic changes in such relatively simple variables as rainfall, wind velocity, and temperature. These may in turn lead to rather complex fluctuations in floral and faunal composition, including disease agents and their carriers. Such fluctuations may include changes in both numbers and types of organisms. Variations of this type occur even in relatively stable environments; even those upon which man has asserted a considerable mastery.

The strategy developed by a population operates to a greater or lesser degree to maximize adaptation through the potential range of variation in environmental parameters. Unexpected, relatively nonperi-

odic changes also occur in the environment. Therefore, good population strategies must be flexible
enough to produce adaptive shifts. While this flexibility may reduce synchronic efficiency under "normal" environmental conditions, it may become adaptive when a sudden change occurs in environmental
parameters. One source of such flexibility may be
poor copying of standard behavior. In strictly biological terms this would be analogous to genetic load, a
concept which may be employed to stress the relationship between synchronically maladaptive traits
and potential adaptation to new environmental conditions.

Populations may have an adverse effect on the
environment in which they are imbedded. That is,
the carrying capacity of the environment may be
threatened through degradation. "Good" strategies,
therefore, must also maintain a diachronic balance
between the population and the environment so that
a relatively stable relationship develops between
game players. Changes in productivity which increase carrying capacity must not lead to environmental degradation if they are to be successful over
the long run.

The game of adaptation is one in which both biological and cultural variables play a part. The task of
analyzing such a game involves the study of specific
encounters between populations and their environments with the ultimate aim of discovering general
rules capable of generating specific strategies.

The growing discipline of medical anthropology
provides an entry point for the study of this problem.
Medical anthropologists focus their attention on pat-

terns of disease and treatment within a wide range of populations and environmental settings. They investigate relationships between behavior and epidemiological patterns and are frequently called upon to aid in the analysis of specific etiological problems. Many, if not all, epidemiological patterns involve complex relationships among physiological, genetic, cultural, demographic, and environmental variables. Intensive field studies as well as cross cultural analyses of behavior related to productivity on the one hand and epidemiology on the other should prove highly useful for the analysis of the adaptive process.

The investigation of human adaptation must focus on the mechanisms involved in both negative feedback, which preserves systemic balance, and positive feedback, which is involved in the process of change. Both types of feedback involve cyclical interactions between biobehavioral systems and the environment. For the human species, in which culture plays the most significant role in adaptation, one must investigate relationships between the environment, cognitive patterns, and adjustive responses.

My theoretical bias is tied to the biological theory of evolution. It is my strong conviction that the evolution of human behavior, including what has come to be called culture history, can best be understood in terms of such a theory. My major debt therefore, is to Darwin and modern theoretical biology, although the work of social evolutionists has also had an important influence on my thinking. My differences with the latter group are discussed in detail in Chapter 2.

This book is an attempt to show how some of the

materials and techniques of medical anthropology can be used to integrate data on human behavior into an evolutionary framework. It does not present the entire field of medical anthropology. I hope that my colleagues as well as debutants in this discipline will find my approach useful. It is at the anthropological community at large, however, that this book is aimed. It is hoped that many of the arguments presented can be extended into subdisciplines other than medical anthropology, and that the overall point of view applies directly to the main stream of anthropological theory.

In the following chapter I stress the applicability of the biological theory of evolution for both physical and cultural anthropology, suggesting, in fact, that a unified approach which has remained one of the strengths of American anthropology can only be maintained through an adherence to the biological theory. In the same chapter I offer criticisms of social evolutionists and the concept of the "superorganic" to which most of them have adhered. The relationship between medical anthropological research and the biological theory of evolution is then explored briefly.

In Chapter 3 I discuss the relationships among a range of biological and cultural phenomena which affect health and disease. Attention is focused on infectious or parasitic diseases, nutritional disorders, and stress.

Chapter 4 offers a hypothesis concerning adaptation to disease and examines various factors relating to behavior and environment which complicate the testing of such a hypothesis. The methods and techniques of historical epidemiology and paleopathology are reviewed in relation to the problem of adaptation.

Chapter 5 is concerned with native medical practice. A distinction is drawn between preventive and therapeutic medicine, and the suggestion is made that preventive medicine is more effective than therapy in primitive society. The underlying hypothesis here is that poor theories tend to retard discovery, but that what we would define as preventive medicine from our own scientific perspective lies outside the realm of medical theory in many non-Western societies. Under such conditions trial and error adjustments, some of which have their origin in random behavior, can become fixed in a behavioral system through the process of reward and punishment. In effect successful strategies can be arrived at through operant conditioning, rather than through some teleological process. The ethnoscientific explanations for such behavior may then come after the fact and may be used to validate and reinforce successful behavior. Thus the explanation becomes ethnically valid but has little or nothing to do with the origin of a particular adaptation.

In Chapter 6 the traditional roles of medical practitioners and ideas about diagnostics are examined. The extension of medicine into nonmedical areas of social behavior is discussed in relation to the hypothesis that the more esoteric a medical system, and/or the higher the incidence of serious disease, the more likely the extension of the practitioner's role beyond the confines of what Westerners would define as strictly medical practice. In addition, an explanation for widespread similarities in the affectual aspects of medical practice is offered. This discussion rests on a comparison of those feedbacks which aid in the discovery of effective cures for physically based disease with those feedbacks which lead to effective treatment for psychosomatic disorders. It is suggested that the clue to such differences lies in the source of information tapped in the therapeutic situation. In the first case the information comes from the ambiguous areas of biological characteristics of diseases (which are variable from patient to patient), and from specific physiological effects of therapeutic agents. In the second case information comes directly from the response of the patient to the social drama played out in the therapeutic situation.

Chapter 6 concludes with some tentative suggestions as to how environmental parameters, particularly prevalent diseases, may affect the development of behavioral systems. The material presented in this chapter is closer to the work traditionally done by medical anthropologists and ethnologists interested in religious systems and witchcraft, but an attempt is made to place the material in the context of the central theoretical arguments of the book.

Chapter 7 deals with the effects of Western medicine on native medical systems. Through the use of material from my own field research, it is suggested that change occurs most easily in those areas of behavior in which analogue models between two different systems exist. This discussion is essential to a full understanding of human behavioral evolution because it highlights a major difference between the mechanisms of somatic change, on the one hand, and cultural change on the other. The point made is that while all somatic change depends ultimately on random mutations, change in human behavioral systems is channeled by certain specifically cultural mechanisms which act to reduce random variation. Such channeling comes from the development of theories (strategies for behavior), experimentation, feedbacks from trial and error, and from the process of diffusion of information from one population to another. As many anthropologists have already pointed out, the process of diffusion is one of the major mechanisms of change in the evolution of human behavioral systems. But to say that a trait has diffused explains nothing. The mechanisms of diffusion must also be explained. The specific point stressed in Chapter 7 is that change is most easily effected when similarities in role systems exist between one society and another. Cultural differences in these basically similar role systems, however, distort behavioral outcomes.

At this point my approach to disease-related behavior as a realm of significant data must be stressed. Recently a good deal of research in and out of medical anthropology has been concerned with so-called folk models, i.e., the analysis of behavioral rules from the perspective of the native system itself. A total concentration on folk medicine per se, whether it be preventive medicine, therapy, or a combination of the two, tends to obscure the ecological relationships which constitute the *real* epidemiological pattern of a population. The fact that the Mano of Liberia do not consider malaria to be a disease because so many people have it does tend to remove malaria from Mano disease theory. But such a belief does not obviate the fact that malaria as a pathological condition

9

has both genetic and behavioral effects on the population. Malaria is known to change gene frequencies, affect the immunological pattern, produce susceptibility to other pathologies, and lower the efficiency of affected individuals, perhaps even in what appear to be subclinical cases. In addition, those areas of behavior which affect the rate of infection and transmission of disease, whether or not they happen to be a part of some native disease theory, are crucial for a thorough analysis of population ecology. Disease patterns may have a covert but real effect on the choice of habitation sites, patterns of social interaction, and economic productivity.

The current tendency in anthropology to stress "ethnoscience" can have the dangerous effect of transforming ecological analyses into a series of ethnological just-so stories. This is particularly true when the researcher fails to observe actual behavior patterns which pertain to a particular set of stated rules. Equally dangerous is the tendency to restrict observations to a single ethnosemantic domain. Disease-related behavior must be treated as more than just a linguistic category.

It is not my intention here to exclude ethnoscience from medical anthropology, however. In fact in later chapters I hope to demonstrate its importance for the construction of an evolutionary model of behavioral adaptation to disease. Both folk models and the behavior which these models generate must be considered, as well as the empirically verifiable relationships between behavior and the specific environment in which any population is embedded.

I am not unaware of the fact that the approach

stressed here has its own peculiar difficulties. It is quite likely that all aspects of behavior have some effect on the epidemiological patterns of a population. Thus if my prescription for research were to be followed literally it would be impossible to exclude any data from the realm of medical anthropology. Specific hypotheses and problems should provide the guidelines for data collection. The problem of disjunction between economic productivity and health, for example, can be examined in terms of a specific set of subsistence techniques. Alternatively, one may choose to concentrate on the effects of stress on such demographic factors as size or distribution of populations. Patterns of diet may be investigated in relation to differential work loads, status, periods of stress, caloric output and input, or even in terms of ecological parameters. Another way out of the dilemma of too much data is to examine human behavior in relation to known facts about the biological requirements of specific disease organisms. In this way basic biological data become a guide for the collection of anthropological material.

All of these suggestions contain hypothetical biases which in fact serve to limit and structure the direction of research. Certain accepted dictums of the scientific method are also involved in the problem of designing a legitimate study. The problem of randomizing data to factor out interfering variables as well as to insure a representative sample is a serious one in all anthropological research, and it is particularly important when a complex series of variables is involved. Good sampling techniques can actually go a long way in the process of simplifying research procedures. On the other hand, the existence of high-speed computers and a wide variety of programs suitable for ecological problems increases the possibility of dealing with highly complex material. Careful structuring of research designs before data collection can help to increase the eventual output, and the use of computers in conjunction with ongoing research can guide or even change the direction of data collection.

A particularly interesting feature of computer research is the possibility of simulating change through time. A simulation program considers basic data plus certain rules of variation which may be manipulated to produce hypothetical variations in the state of the same system. One can vary the conditions of change to produce different effects on the system. In anthropological research the programmer can begin with empirical data on some population and project population and behavioral changes through time. These can be checked empirically against some optimal theoretical model developed with the help of the computer. This type of research has already been carried out by Kunstadter et al. (1963) in determining whether or not the model of prescriptive cross cousin marriage is feasible for an inbreeding population. The program simulated several generations searching out available spouses. The study demonstrated that sufficient eligible relatives could not be expected to occur in each generation. Thus the continuation of such a theoretical system through time is highly improbable. Kunstadter is currently involved in another simulation study in which two competing populations in Thailand will be compared. In this study the computer will judge the effects of two behavioral systems in their environmental settings and predict demographic outcomes for a projected series of generations.

Elsewhere I have suggested that simulation studies might be used to generate most and least optimal environmental conditions for the occurrence of particular culture traits (Alland 1967). The computer would produce a theoretical geographic distribution which could be compared to actual trait distributions. A good match between the predicted and actual distributions would be suggestive of cross cultural behavioral maximizations in relation to specific environmental types. My projected test case would consider the use of human fecal matter as fertilizer. The custom has both positive and negative features in that it produces a health hazard but at the same time increases soil fertility. Factors which would weigh in favor of use would be related to overall soil fertility, availability of land resources, type of agricultural production, certain climatic factors, and high population density.

Certain other modern techniques might prove particularly useful for medical anthropological research. One of the most promising of these is the use of blood for seriological studies. A major limitation of epidemiological field research has been the lack of good clinical data. In my own research in the Ivory Coast I was forced to rely on hospital statistics for estimates of disease incidence. Such statistics are subject to gross error because they represent treated cases only and because diagnoses are often inaccurate. The presence of a doctor in a field research team of course decreases this problem, but medical personnel are not always available, and under most conditions doctors are unable to provide reliable medical histories for a study population. The analysis of blood serum from a well-drawn sample under laboratory conditions is an excellent method for obtaining accurate material on a good part of the disease history of a population. Serum must be collected carefully and immediately frozen, if possible in liquid nitrogen. This need not present great difficulties since collecting techniques are relatively simple, portable equipment exists, and rapid air transportation is now available almost everywhere. While analytic techniques are complicated, there are several competent laboratories in the United States which are extremely anxious to obtain serum samples from widely distributed populations (see Blumberg 1962).

Since particular research projects require their own techniques and methods I do not wish to extend this discussion further except to emphasize the fact that any sound research dealing with ecological variables must be precise and include accurate counting. This should be obvious, but I stress it here because some anthropologists have been content to present models as data, or to give a few exemplary cases to demonstrate a particular point. This kind of presentation begs the question. It is essential that the data used in support of hypotheses be presented accurately and in detail, so as not to foreclose possible alternative explanations.

Ecological analysis in anthropology is in the peculiar position of emerging as a scientific pursuit at the same time that the material for investigation is becoming either scarce or contaminated by the influence of Western technology. This is particularly true in the realm of health and disease, since many governmental, international, and religious institutions have embarked recently upon a medical crusade of world-wide proportions. Local methods of population control and "native" diets are particularly susceptible to influence from the outside. In addition, rapid changes in demographic structure, which are the frequent outcome of improved medical conditions or technological change, markedly affect the genetic constitution of a population. Relatively isolated populations present the most interesting data for research relating to environmental adaptation, and it is these groups which are disappearing most rapidly. Adequate and accurate data for internal as well as cross cultural analysis must be gathered in the near future or be forever lost.

The discussion which follows demands a certain familiarity with technical terms from medicine and epidemiology. Most of these have standard definitions, but some, including "health" and "disease," are either ambiguous or are defined differently by different authors. In addition, it is quite likely that a few readers will find themselves unfamiliar with the biology of disease organisms. Therefore the remainder of this chapter will be devoted to an outline of basic definitions and a short introduction to the major types of human parasite. Those whose training carries them beyond this simple and abbreviated discussion should skip to Chapter 2.

INTRODUCTION

Relatively standard definitions of medical terms may be found in any medical dictionary, but in the case of "illness" and "health" one might well consult the thirteen-volume *The Complete Oxford Dictionary of the English Language.* The connotations which encumber these terms in English reveal a metaphysical orientation which was, and in many cases still is, attached to such concepts in our own behavioral system. Under disease one finds:

1. To deprive of ease, make uneasy, to put to discomfort, to trouble, annoy, incommode, molest.
2. To bring into morbid or unhealthy condition; to cause illness, sickness or disease in, to infect with disease.

Illness is defined as:

1. The condition of being ill. Bad moral quality, condition of wickedness, depravity, evil conduct, condition of character.
2. Unpleasantness, disagreeableness, troublesomeness, hurtfulness, noxiousness, badness.
3. Bad or unhealthy condition of the body, the condition of being ill.

Ill is defined as:

1. Morally evil, wicked, iniquitous, depraved, vicious, immoral, blameworthy, reprehensible.
2. Marked by evil intent, or by want of good feelings, malevolent, hostile, unfriendly, adverse, unkind, harsh, cruel, hurtful, injurious, pernicious, noxious, mischievous, prejudicial, dangerous.

On the other hand "health" is a relatively neutral term:

1. Soundness of body; the condition in which its functions are duly and efficiently discharged.
2. By extension, the general condition of the body with respect to the efficient or inefficient discharge of functions.

Two polar concepts appear to operate in these definitions. On the one hand, illness as a condition is caused by some agent acting on the individual in a willful way to upset the "efficient discharge of functions." On the other hand, illness itself is a kind of evil which emanates from within the affected person. To be ill is to act in some way against others. Contagion and contamination with evil are intertwined, and illness becomes the manifestation of some inner force. Disease is a corruption of the body, and by extension a corruption of the spirit.

As one might expect, by the antiquity of these concepts, they are at least partially at variance with the germ theory of disease. The idea of contagion (which predates the germ theory) is wide-spread in non-Western societies and has the frequent effect of separating the sick from the healthy. Quarantine as an effective method of prevention far outdates other techniques of preventive medicine. The relationship between disease and evil creates an isomorphism between folk beliefs and modern medical practice and acts to limit the spread of certain diseases.

It is probable that the concept of external disease agents has developed from the frequent discovery that specific external conditions can be readily associated with disease. Once such agents or conditions become part of a belief system, effective therapeutic methods may be sought to purge the afflicted individual.

The fact that many of the concepts inherent in the English definitions are widespread in non-Western medical systems suggests that certain fundamental medical discoveries have been made outside the scope of scientific medicine. These discoveries come to be incorporated in folk theories which develop as explanations of phenomena encountered in the world of experience. They contain many nonempirical elements as well. Such folk theories influence the direction and scope of perception, and therefore they play an important, if sometimes rearguard, action in the series of encounters which comprise the continuing game of behavioral adaptation. The germ theory and the scientific method go far beyond the possibilities inherent in any prescientific medical system.

It might appear strange therefore that modern definitions of health and disease are still either ambiguous or limited in scope. Disease is defined most comfortably, particularly for ecological studies, in terms of specific conditions (symptoms and suspected agents) rather than in more general terms (as some abstract concept). Health becomes a residue category for the absence of disease, and few medical specialists would care to attempt a description of "the perfectly healthy individual."

While other epidemiological terms are more precise, certain difficulties arise when they are applied in an absolute sense. The definitions offered here are in keeping with those generally accepted by the medical profession and will be adhered to in later chapters.

Diseases may be categorized in terms of duration. A *chronic* disease is one which persists through a considerable period of time, often but not always at a particular level of incapacitation. Certain chronic diseases terminate in the death of the individual affected; others lead to complications unrelated to the original condition. Still others may persist for many years without producing mortality. Arthritis, leprosy, syphilis, and many heart conditions are chronic diseases. An *acute* disease is one of rapid development and short duration. Acute diseases may be mild (the common cold) or severe (pneumonia).

Contagious diseases, also known as *communicable* diseases, are those which can be transmitted directly from host to host without some intervening organism, such as a biting insect.

Diseases are also classified in terms of the type of agent involved in their etiology.

Infectious or *parasitic* diseases are caused by some living biotic agent which produces morbid (disease) symptoms in the host.

Functional disorders are caused by some physical strain on the system of the affected individual, e.g., osteo-arthritis. Such disorders may result from long-term wear and tear on the system or from what Selye describes as the "stress syndrome." This involves the response of the neuro-endocrine system to various irritations, including physical or emotional trauma, the secondary effects of infectious disease, or dietary imbalance (see Chapter 3).

INTRODUCTION

Genetic disease is the result of some inborn "error of metabolism" such as a malfunctioning pancreas, which may produce diabetes.

Nutritional disease is caused by some dietary deficiency such as hypovitaminosis, protein malnutrition or, in some cases, an overdose of a particular nutritional element.

Psychosomatic disease develops from psychological problems in the life of an affected individual. Although its actual etiology is incompletely understood, some psychosomatic disease may be related to traumatic conditions in which psychological disturbances alter endocrine function.

Diseases which persist in a population are said to be *endemic* in that population. If a disease attacks periodically in the same geographic zone it is said to be *epidemic*. Epidemics usually occur within a temporally limited period, spread rapidly through a population, and then disappear. Sometimes, however, diseases which are endemic in a population increase to epidemic proportions. In some cases the endemic form of a disease is somewhat different in its symptomology and severity than the epidemic form.

Diseases which occur in animal populations may be either *enzootic* (endemic) or *epizootic* (epidemic), depending upon whether the rate of infection in the total population is low or high.

The terms epidemic, endemic, enzootic, and epizootic are flexible. The rate of infection which is taken as sufficient for an epidemic (or epizootic) may vary according to the particular disease in question. Thus only a few cases per thousand population of

20

viral encephalitis mark an "epidemic," while the rate of infected individuals per thousand for measles must be quite high before the disease reaches epidemic proportions.

Diseases may be transferred to man from an animal population which acts as a *reservoir*. The reservoir for yellow fever, for example, consists of monkeys living in the forest zone surrounding settlements in Africa and South America. Such animals are often infected with a form of the disease known as jungle yellow fever but identical to the human form of the disease. Other organisms may act as disease *vectors*, carrying parasites from lower animals to man, and from man to man. In some cases vector organisms, such as houseflies, operate as mechanical carriers of parasites. In many other cases the parasite completes part of its life cycle in the vector. This is true for the agent of schistosomiasis which must pass through certain species of snail, of the malaria parasite, which spends part of its life cycle in various but specific species of *anophelene* mosquitoes, and the trypanosome of sleeping sickness which develops in the tsetse fly. On some occasions human beings act as hosts for particular disease organisms and yet display no visible signs of pathology. These, nevertheless, may be *carriers* who infect other members of the population.

Epidemiologists use a few special terms to designate certain phenomena associated with the demography of health and disease. Among the most important of these are:

Morbidity: The rate of incidence of a particular disease (the number of cases of a disease per unit of population in a given unit of time).

Mortality: The rate of deaths due to a set of causes or a particular cause (the number of deaths per unit of population in a given unit of time).

Fecundity: The ability to produce offspring.

Fertility: The number of children produced by a defined group of women (usually per thousand of population) over a defined period of time (usually one year).

Demographic data may characterize an entire population or specify some group within it. Thus the crude birth rate represents the number of children born per one thousand of population per year, while an adjusted birth rate may represent the number of children born per thousand women of childbearing age in one year. Death rates may be crude, referring to all causes in an entire population or adjusted to some disease, social class, age group, or to sex. Each type of statistic describes an aspect of a population, but it should be obvious that what is being described in each case is quite different.

Epidemiologists often document the frequency with which some disease occurs in a population within a specific time period. This is referred to as the *incidence* of the disease and is the same as morbidity. On the other hand, the epidemiologist may be interested in describing or designating the proportion of individuals in a population who have a particular disease at one point in time. This is referred to as *prevalence*.

Immunity runs the gamut from *partial* to *total* resistance to disease. It may be *specific* for particular diseases or *general* for a wide range of conditions.

Immunity may be *inherited* or *acquired.* The latter results either from a disease episode or through inoculation and may be *temporary or permanent.* A temporary immunity to certain conditions may be passed through breast milk from a nursing mother to her offspring.

Man acts as the host for a wide variety of parasites. These fall into several distinctive groups on the phylogenetic scale. Beginning with the simplest and moving upward in biological complexity, these organisms include viruses, bacteria and other fungi, protozoa, helminths (worms) of various types, and arthropods or insects.

The viruses constitute a large group of submicroscopic organisms which reproduce only through active chemical resynthesis in the cells of the host. Thus in effect all viruses are parasitic. Not all of them attack man, however, and the diseases they do produce vary in severity from the common cold to smallpox.

A peculiar feature of some viruses is their slow activity. Certain pathological species may not attack the cells of a host organism for a considerable period. This latency may persist indefinitely, and then, for some reason as yet unknown, the character of the virus may change. It then begins an active reproductive phase and produces morbid symptoms. Recently a series of diseases have been discovered in animals and man in which the responsible virus acts very slowly. The incubation period in these diseases may vary from several months to several years before the onset of visible symptoms, and then the diseases may become rapidly acute or develop into a chronic syndrome. One of these "slow virus" diseases, Kuru, is

23

limited in distribution to a small population in Highland New Guinea. Kuru is a disease of the central nervous system. Its incubation period lasts from about eighteen months to two years, after which nervous degeneration is rapid. This is followed by death within one year of the onset of the first symptoms.

Medical specialists are now investigating the possibility that a rather impressive series of diseases which were once thought to be genetic in nature are actually caused by slow viruses. Among these are multiple sclerosis and muscular dystrophy. The long incubation period and the possibility that such parasites might be passed down from mother to offspring could create an understandable confusion between theories of genetic and viral origin for these diseases.

A wide variety of antibody-containing serums have been developed for viral diseases. In most cases, it is quite easy to produce an attenuated virus capable of producing an immune response. The duration of immunity varies from disease to disease. The major difficulty in producing serums against viral diseases has been the isolation and reproduction of viral organisms outside their specific hosts. Recently a great deal of progress has been made with growth in tissue cultures. The intriguing possibility exists that many, if not all, forms of cancer are caused by slow viruses. If this is the case, it perhaps will be possible to develop antisera against cancer.

With a few notable exceptions, effective treatments for viral diseases have not been developed. It is therefore necessary to employ preventive therapy to limit the spread of most such conditions. Major efforts in

this regard have been made with smallpox, poliomyelitis, and yellow fever.

It is difficult to characterize bacterial organisms
since they range widely in pathogeneity and in biotic
requirements both inside and outside their hosts.
These one-celled organisms are generally grouped
into three major morphological types: *cocci*, or round
forms; *bacilli*, or rod forms; and *spirochete*, or spiral
forms. Both cocci and bacilli may occur in chains
(*streptococci* or *streptobacilli*). In addition, cocci may
also appear in bunches or *staphylococci*. Bacteria are
also classified according to the kind of media they
grow on, the texture and color of their colonies, and
the type of chemical reactions they produce in the
media. A highly useful device has been developed for
the identification of bacterial organisms. It consists
of a staining process (*gram staining*) in which some
organisms exhibit the ability to resist stain (*gram
negative*) while others stain easily (*gram positive*).
Gram negative and positive organisms tend to respond differently to various types of antibiotic therapy. Some bacteria are protected with a waxy coat
(tuberculosis, for example) which renders them somewhat resistant to desiccation; others (such as tetanus)
may pass into a dormant state, forming spores, when
not in their hosts.

Some bacteria require a medium completely devoid
of oxygen for their growth. These *anaerobic* organisms must penetrate deeply into host tissue before
they can reproduce and generate pathological symptoms. Both tentanus and gas gangrene are caused by
organisms of this type. Several bacterial organisms
are highly tissue specific, particularly those of vene-

25

real disease, while others may attack the host at several points, for example, *Mycrococcus pyogenes* var. *areus*. This parasite generally inhabits human skin and may produce no pathological conditions. If, however, the host's resistance is lowered and if the organism gains access to subcutaneous tissue, boils may result. When the same organism invades the deep tissue of a susceptible host it may attack on a wide scale, producing localized infections of the bones, heart, brain, or other organs, or a generalized blood poisoning.

Although the human body produces a long-lasting or permanent immunity to many viral diseases (the common cold and influenza are frequently encountered exceptions), only a few bacteria stimulate such an immune response. Few successful antisera for bacterial diseases have been produced. On the other hand, most bacteria are highly susceptible to various forms of chemical and antibiotic therapy.

Most fungus diseases attack the skin and are little more than annoying. This is not always true, however. A few fungi cause mild to severe respiratory ailments, the most widely known of which is histoplasmosis, a condition fairly common in the United States. Other fungus parasites may cause gross damage to the mucous membranes and one, Madura foot, found in Africa, produces irreversible changes in the tissue which may prove fatal if not treated through radical amputation of the affected parts. The one characteristic which almost all fungus diseases share is their extreme refractoriness to treatment. While many fungus diseases can be controlled, they are extremely difficult to cure.

26

Some of the most troublesome human pathologies are caused by protozoa (one-celled animals). Perhaps the most widely known of these are the parasites of malaria and African sleeping sickness. Many protozoa (the amoeba of amoebic dysentery is one exception) must pass part of their life cycle in some vector organism, often an insect, and one of the major methods of prevention consists in destroying the vector. This is particularly important because until recently few really effective therapeutic methods existed for the treatment of protozoan diseases. Even now many of the chemotherapeutic agents produce a toxic response in the host.

Helminths of various types, particularly *nematodes*, or round worms, and *platyhelminthenes*, or flat worms, also have proved very troublesome for human populations. Like the protozoa, many helminths are obliged to pass a part of their developmental cycle in a vector organism. While most of these are insects, snails and various crustacea also serve this purpose. In most cases each type of vector is specific to a particular species of parasite. Many helminths are injected directly into the host by the bite of the vector, but some gain entry through the mouth. Others pass directly through the skin (schistosomiasis). Helminthic diseases are perhaps the most difficult to treat. These parasites, like protozoa, have become highly specialized to the biology of their hosts, and many therapeutic techniques produce debilitating responses in an infected individual. Again until recently the only effective measures against helminths have been attacks on the vector organisms. In many cases the vectors prove to be as difficult to control as the parasites which they carry. When this obtains, the only effective measure has been to remove human beings from contact with them.

Most but by no means all protozoan and helminthic diseases are tropical or semitropical in distribution. This is because the parasite or the vector or both require a tropical environment with high temperature and humidity for survival. The label "tropical disease" must be approached with caution, however. Many diseases are tropical only in the sense that the world's underdeveloped areas coincide with the tropics (see Ackerknecht 1966). Such areas generally have rather primitive sanitary facilities and poor standards of public health. Many "tropical" diseases in historical perspective have had temperate distributions as well. Malaria and yellow fever were, for example, known as far north as Connecticut in the United States. Leprosy and malaria were quite prevalent in northern Europe until relatively recent times.

In addition to the pathogens discussed above, a certain number of arthropods act as ectoparasites on man and his domestic animals. Under normal conditions these produce only minimal damage, but almost all ectoparasites are also potential carriers of disease organisms. Fleas, mites, and ticks carry typhus and related diseases; fleas carry plague; mosquitoes carry yellow fever, malaria, virus encephalitis, various helminths, dengue fever, and countless other viruses. The tsetse fly carries the trypanosomes of African sleeping sickness; the South American form is carried by a beetle. The sand fly (*phlebotomus*) carries various forms of leishmaniasis.

INTRODUCTION

Man is surrounded by a microscopic and submicroscopic world capable of inflicting great damage on him as well as on his domestic animals and plants. The struggle for survival includes frequent combat as well as accommodation with these organisms.

CHAPTER 2

EVOLUTIONARY THEORY

Evolutionary theory has once more become an active force in the development of anthropology, but the question remains: Which theory of evolution? While Darwinian analogues abound, when it comes down to theoretical statements and empirical strategies concerned with "social" or "cultural" evolution, the departures from the biological model are rather startling. There are several reasons for these departures.

Most social or cultural evolutionists, be they multilineal or unilineal, have focused on the outcomes or products of evolution. They have thus neglected the mechanisms which produce change and the processes involved in adaptation. Tylor (1871) and particularly Childe (1936) are the only social evolutionists who have come to grips with one aspect of process, namely diffusion, and even they did not give much thought to its mechanics. Yet the biological model stresses process and mechanics rather than outcome.

Campbell (1965) has presented an important elaboration of Keller's variation and selective retention model of social change. Such a model stresses the random nature of variation and accounts for directional change or adaptive fit on the basis of selective retention, a process which provides a perfect analogy with natural selection. Campbell, however, sees disanalogies between cultural and biological evolution in the areas of specific mechanisms of variation and retention, the modes of transmission, and the measurement of adaptive change. I hope to show below that while these disanalogies represent important divergences from biological mechanisms, they in no way force abandonment of Darwinian theory in problems of cultural evolution. I think also that Campbell's unwillingness to use the standard measure of adaptation (a coefficient of selection based on comparative fertility) draws him unnecessarily away from the biological model.

Sahlins and Service (1960) have derived two laws of process: the law of cultural dominance and the law of evolutionary potential. These are clearly drawn from biological theory, but they are imbedded in what is essentially a nonbiological model, and the authors provide no biological measure of adaptation.[1]

[1] The law of cultural dominance is based on the biological principle that general dominance (high comparative efficiency) leads to greater all-round adaptability. The law states: "That cultural system which more effectively exploits the energy resources of a given environment will tend to spread in that environment at the expense of less effective systems." (Sahlins and Service 1960: 75)

The law of evolutionary potential states that less specialized cultures have a greater potential for change than those which are highly specialized or rigidly niche

31

EVOLUTIONARY THEORY

The concept of the superorganic, as defined by Kroeber (1952), White (1959), or Steward (1958), creates a barrier between man's biological and cultural development which has only partially been removed by the work of Washburn (1959), Geertz (1962), Hallowell (1955), Wallace (1961), Dobzhansky (1962), and Fox and Tiger (1966). White's assumption that culture causes culture, and that change occurs on the level of the superorganic, is in conflict with the facts of biological change which occurs somatically at the organismic level. Unless this conflict can be resolved or eliminated, the biological model can have only a limited significance for cultural evolution.

Perhaps the most important divergence from Darwinian theory has been the neglect of environmental factors in evolution. This deletion of a major portion of Darwin's argument begins with the early evolutionists, particularly Morgan (1877), who created models of unilineal development.[2] If the development of culture is a unilineal process, the effects of local environments must by definition be irrelevant. To make such theories work, some driving force must be substituted for the environment as a selecting

---

adapted. This law is drawn directly from Darwinian theory in which cladogenic lines are expected to derive from a generalized stock, new to a particular environmental niche, rather than from a stable, highly specialized species.

[2] Morgan was not completely unaware of environmental pressures. In *Ancient Society* he distinguishes between the development of neolithic cultures in Europe and the New World on the basis of the availability of animals suitable for domestication. Nonetheless, his scheme is essentially unilineal and must consequently ignore the selective effects of the environment.

32

agent. This force may be a teleological law of nature (Spencer 1864) which carries all matter from the simple to the complex, from the unordered to the highly ordered. This might be called the anti-entropic theory of evolution in which neg-entropy is taken as some mystical property of matter.

The development of complexity is, of course, a question of structural priorities. Certain structures can only develop out of a series of precedent forms. But such development cannot be explained as some automatic process. Spencer also saw evolutionary development in terms of the competitive nature of organisms, and it was he who coined the phrase "survival of the fittest." But this concept, while it is central to Darwinian selection, ignores the role of environment as the selecting agent. Of course organisms compete but in an environmental context. Which organisms are fit depends on their accommodation to specific environmental demands.

Modern unilineal evolutionists, with the exception of Childe (1936, 1951), continue to ignore the environment or relegate it to the role of selective agent in what is referred to as "specific evolution" (Sahlins and Service 1960). These scholars make a distinction between "culture" and "cultures." Their arguments are backed up, perhaps inadvertently, by some biologists and physical anthropologists, who either see evolution as a series of progressive outcomes (Huxley 1943), or who view culture itself as an environmental niche (Brace and Montagu 1966).

Steward's (1958) distinction between organic and superorganic environments, borrowed, of course, from other scholars, also places the burden of selec-

33

tion on culture as the crucial "environment." There is some truth in this. Morgan, Maine, and Marx all saw valid connections between the development of social forms and the institution of property, whereas Marx also stressed relationships between modes of production and social institutions. But for analytic reasons I would prefer to view culture as adaptive response to environmental pressures. Man changes his environment, often drastically, through the adaptive mechanism of culture, and this changed environment then acts as a selective agent on man's physical structure as well as on his behavior. This line of reasoning is crucial if we are to retain the biological model of evolution in its pure form.

The role of the environment must not be exaggerated in explanations of cultural development. Environment is a selecting agent and not an active force itself capable of producing change. This distinction becomes clear if we compare the arguments surrounding environmental determinism with evolutionary theory. Environmental determinists believe that the occurrence of particular traits can be explained causally in relation to specific environmental demands. Their case is destroyed by the existence of several cultural traditions within the same environmental context. Thus it might be said that aborigines and sheep farmers in the desert of Australia exploit their local environments in such contrasting ways that it would be unreasonable to assume that environmental pressures act in any meaningful way to determine cultural processes. When this argument is turned against evolutionists, however, it becomes an attack on a straw man. No evolutionist is a determinist in the above sense because in Darwinian theory novel forms develop on the level of individual organisms. These forms are then exposed to the selection pressure of the specific environment in which they occur. Whether or not new traits are to become fixed in a population depends upon their fitness within their environmental setting.

Evolution must be taken as an opportunistic process. Environmental selection works on what is there. Although parallels may develop in the same or in related environmental contexts, the selective process will, in general, have different effects on different systems (see Gadjusek 1964). Aboriginal hunters and Australian sheep farmers represent different adaptive modes. If these two systems are not in direct competition, selective forces will operate on them in different ways. The first question to be asked then is: What are the differences between Australian sheep farming techniques and sheep farming techniques in England, the original home of the Australian farmers? For these farmers represent the adaptation of an old form to a new environment. If adequate historical and/or archaeological material were available, the same question could be asked about the behavior of Australian hunters in comparison to the behavior of their ancestors in some former habitat from which it must be assumed they migrated.

If, as may be the case, the two populations under consideration are in competition, the second question to be asked is: Which system of behavior is most adaptive in this particular environmental setting? It would seem obvious that the sheep farmer has the advantage. He is able to extract more than the hunter

35

from the environment and therefore can support a larger population on the land. But even this conclusion must be approached with caution. Through a long time span it might turn out that domestic animals are so destructive to the marginal conditions of the Australian desert that the land will have to be abandoned to the original (and less energy producing) hunting population.

In the short run, i.e., from generation to generation, adaptation can be measured simply on the basis of selective coefficients which reflect reproductive success. The evolutionist, however, might wish to predict the staying power of a population through time. Naturally occurring environmental change is a major factor in extinction. Its effect may be taken as gratuitous, but populations themselves change environmental conditions. For a specific set of adaptations there is a level beyond which the extraction of energy from the environment may create irreversible changes which are inimical to survival. The maximum population load beyond which such change will occur is referred to as the carrying capacity. The carrying capacity of an environment is dependent upon natural conditions and the exploitative techniques of the species inhabiting it.

Among species, man is the most able to alter these techniques. Throughout the history of the human species technological change has increased the carrying capacity of specific environments for human populations. There are instances, however, which demonstrate that man may exceed the carrying capacity of a particular geographic zone and degrade it to such a degree that, short of a complete shift in technology, the carrying capacity is significantly reduced. This is the typical outcome of overgrazing which results in the production of man-made deserts. In many cases, as maximal carrying capacity is approached, Malthusian checks on the population begin to operate. When this happens the population may be stabilized and environmental degradation prevented.

The human species has been particularly destructive, especially in recent times. This is due partially to the result of rapid and spectacular technological innovations and partially to the development of death control through modern medicine. Evolutionary studies of human populations, particularly those concerned with relatively stable systems (homeostatic adjustments to the environment), must consider carrying capacity. The important questions are: How close to optimal is the population size in relation to the carrying capacity? Are there mechanisms (including but not necessarily exclusively Malthusian controls) which prevent expansion of the population beyond the carrying capacity? How does technological change tend to change the carrying capacity, and what long-range effects will it have on the stability of the environment?

All these questions depend on the ability of the researcher to make adequate estimates of carrying capacity. This is a particularly important and difficult problem for anthropologists. These estimates must include such environmental variables as soil type, minimal fallow period, temperature, rainfall, evapotranspiration, erosion, prevalent diseases, and such cultural factors as settlement patterns, mode of production, disposal of wastes, use of fertilizers, irrigation, trade, and taboos on particular foods.

The staying power of culture, however, is not to

be taken as a measure of adaptation. Individuals are the bearers of culture just as they are the bearers of genes. The assumption is that in the long run, if carrying capacity is exceeded, numbers will be reduced. Therefore carrying capacity is a concept which helps the evolutionist make long-range predictions about adaptation or, conversely, the extinction of particular systems.

It is interesting that a line of reasoning quite different from that of the unilineal evolutionists has led to an almost equally consistent neglect of the environment as a selective agent in the development of human behavioral systems. This view is most clearly expressed by Murdock (1949). Murdock's statement of evolution is totally nonlinear. The process is seen rather as a series of adjustments to internal conditions which occur within particular types of social systems. Imbalances between residence and marriage rules, and systems of terminology, lead to regular changes which in turn lead to further imbalances, and so on. Murdock is aware that environmental pressures have some effect on the development of social systems (Murdock 1955, 1959a), but his major interest, justifiably, has always been focused on adjustments which develop within systems. This approach has led Murdock toward the development of a tool for ethnohistorical analysis which he has applied in his book *Africa* (1959b). A similar technique has been employed by Eggan, most recently in *The American Indian* (1966).

Steward (1937, 1958) and again Eggan (1966) have examined the relationships between ecological factors and the development of social-structural change, but they have tended to emphasize what they consider to be a direct *causal* relationship between the environment and a particular form of social structure (see Vayda and Rappaport 1968). This point of view represents a kind of watered-down environmental determinism and is unsound because evolution, as has already been pointed out, is opportunistic, acting on a set of existing or emerging properties. It is a Markov chain process containing elements of indeterminancy which must be considered.

Other analysts, from Rivers (1914) and from Radcliffe-Brown (1952), on the one hand, to Levi-Strauss (1949) and Needham (1960), on the other, have concentrated on the effects of "structure on structure." These scholars have pursued a program similiar in some ways to that of Murdock, but they are more restricted in their focus, since they exclude psychological factors from the system to be analyzed, and they display little fondness for ethnohistory, much less evolution.

In spite of this general orientation, Radcliffe-Brown saw the development of social structure as an adaptive process and it is, I think, appropriate to quote his statement on this topic:

Adaptation. This is a key concept of the theory of evolution. It is or can be applied both to the study of the forms of organic life and to the forms of social life amongst human beings. A living organism exists and continues to exist only if it is both internally and externally adapted. The internal adaptation depends on the adjustment of the various organs and their activities, so that the various physiological processes constitute a continuing functioning system by which the life of the organism is maintained. The external adaptation is that of the organism to the environment within which it lives. The distinction of external and internal adaptation is merely a way of distinguishing two aspects of the adaptational system which is the same for organisms of a single species.

When we examine a form of social life amongst human beings as an adaptational system it is useful to distinguish three aspects of the total system . . . ecological . . . social . . . and . . . cultural. . . . What must be emphasized is that these modes of adaptation are only different aspects from which the total adaptational system can be looked at for convenience of analysis and comparison. (Radcliffe-Brown 1952:8-9)

The understanding that this author had of the evolutionary process is supported by the modern biological evolutionary theory. It is noteworthy that Morris Goodman (1963) has structured his theoretical discussion of primate evolution in almost the same terms as those employed by Radcliffe-Brown. Goodman points out that there are two kinds of adaptation, inward directed and outward directed. Inward-directed adaptation is a process related to the development of consistency within the structures of homeostatic systems. Outward-directed adaptation is the outcome of selective encounters between the organism and the environment. Goodman sees the genotypic outcomes of these two types of adaptation as sometimes contradictory (inward-directed adaptation favors homozygosity; outward-directed adaptation favors heterozygosity), but they are taken as part of the same process, i.e., the development of better self-regulating systems in the context of specific environments.

The term adaptation itself must be taken in two senses. The evolutionist views adaptation as a long-range, transgenerational process in which systems develop homeostatic capacities in relation to specific environments. Physiologists, on the other hand, view adaptation as a short-run process of homeostatic adjustment in which individual organisms meet fluctuations in environmental conditions. The physiologist is aware that these systems evolve but his major concern is with their operation.

If these various aspects of adaptation are taken into account, it should not be difficult to sort out a series of connections between evolutionary studies and various types of anthropological analysis. Evolutionary events consist of the development of self-consistent, self-regulating systems (internal adaptation), of fluctuations in systemic variables as they respond to short-term variations in the environmental field (the link between internal and external adaptation), and of long-term anagenic (linear) and cladogenic (branching) transformations in systems as they change in the direction of better environmental fit (external adaptation).

Structural analysis, concerned as it is with the internal logic of systems, is clearly equivalent to the investigation of internal adaptation. Internal adaptation has also been one of the concerns of unilineal evolutionists for what they present in essence is a series of "functional" analyses set in a long-range diachronic and anagenic framework. It is also possible to study the internal adaptation of behavioral systems over shorter runs of time. The analysis of covariance within self-regulating systems (Collins 1965, Vayda and Rappaport 1968, Rappaport 1968) is a powerful tool for the investigation of homeostasis in behavioral systems as they respond to changes in environmental parameters. Such a method is particularly valuable because it avoids the pitfalls of earlier functional analyses (see Nagel 1961, Hempel 1959). External adaptation is best studied through cross cultural analysis and archaeology, through which questions of parallel evolution can be tested. Eggan's (1954) method of controlled comparisons may be used to link internal and external adaptation together in a diachronic framework.

As long as any one of these approaches is taken by its adherents as the key to all anthropological problems, the unity which underlies them all will remain obscured. In addition, the links which must exist between biological processes and cultural evolution will continue to evade understanding. On the other hand, if biological and cultural variables are seen within the context of a single process, then we shall be able to draw freely upon data from all the subdisciplines of anthropology.

To remain true to the Darwinian model of evolutionary theory, and I contend that it is essential to do so, the method used to measure adaptation must be consistently applied. This measure is simply that of selective coefficients based on comparative intra- or interpopulation ratios. In biology a given gene is said to be adaptive for a population if its selective value is higher than that of some other gene affecting the same trait complex. Selective value is measured in terms of the number of offsprings reaching the age of reproduction; organisms carrying the adaptive gene have a higher fertility ratio than organisms carrying the less effective allele. In addition, one species may

42

be said to be better adapted than another if it out-reproduces or replaces the other (which must be a competing species) in the same environmental niche. In general, niches are occupied only by single species, and selection operates within populations of the same species. Organisms which are better adapted in terms of homeostatic mechanisms will be expected to out-reproduce less well-adapted organisms, and the study of homeostatic systems becomes a part of the overall study of evolutionary process.

Energy conservation is one result of efficient homeostasis. Increases in the efficient utilization of energy in all animal populations, including the human species, may lead to increased population, that is, more efficient systems raise the level of Malthusian checks upon maximum population. As far as human behavioral systems are concerned, those which represent more efficient adaptations within a specific environment should demonstrate this adaptation in terms of increased population growth. Thus as man increases the carrying capacity of an environment he also increases his population potential for that environment. V. G. Childe (1938) was, I am sure, aware of this, and he was wise to choose population growth as a measure of evolution and reserve new modes of production for the role of adaptive mechanisms.[3]

[3] The intellectual capacities of man render him capable of limiting population size for other than survival reasons. In the future it is possible that even esthetic considerations might affect conscious attempts at population control. This does not negate the fact, however, that Malthusian pressures do have their consequences for the human species and that the concept of the selective co-efficient can be used as a measure of adaptation.

Sociality coupled with the nonsomatic transmission of cultural traits has specific consequences for the process of human biocultural evolution. Adaptive traits (or maladaptive traits for that matter) may spread across the boundaries of specific populations through diffusion. On the other hand, populations as biological entities may be absorbed into other populations through assimilation. This may produce an extinction of culture traits without a concomitant extinction of individuals. An increase in the number of trait carriers due to the diffusion of a trait should not be confused with an increase due to higher fertility. Maladaptive traits may in some cases spread from population to population and thus produce a net gain. In the long run, however, such traits must lead to a reduction in numbers.

Human populations as social entities may benefit from the combined talents of individual members. Adaptive culture traits, such as medical knowledge and superior economic or military skill, may be held by a minority of individuals and still constitute part of a cultural tradition which contributes significantly to the survival of the entire group. Although I would prefer to eliminate the term entirely, it is in this sense, and this sense only, that the concept of the superorganic is valid.

It is because of the nonsomatic nature of cultural transmission and the facts of human sociality that the extremely controversial concept of group selection probably applies to many specific instances of human biocultural evolution (Williams 1966).

The process of competition between groups provides a relatively simple model for human evolution.

44

Better-adapted populations out-reproduce, assimilate, or, on occasion, destroy their competitors. Evolutionary change, however, takes place within populations (although I am not suggesting that this ever occurs in a vacuum). Here the nonsomatic nature of cultural transmission creates special problems, some of which may bring us dangerously close to social Darwinism, a concept which does not deserve resurrection. While fertility differences between individuals of the same population may sometimes be used to account for the distribution and frequency of specific culture traits, this is often not the case. In addition, one must be very cautious in defining traits, determining what kind of traits are to be dealt with and how to study their relation to adaptation. The following trait classes, for example, are not equivalent: (1) A garden or a fortune, both of which may be inherited socially, depending upon custom. (2) A specific behavior or technique involving skill which may be inherited through learning. (3) A position in the social structure which may be inherited or appointed, ascribed or achieved. (It must be remembered as well that the probability of access to an achieved status can be inherited.)

The pitfalls inherent in dealing with such trait classes can be avoided, I think, by returning to the biological model. Related behavioral traits, that is, those which apply to the same problem of adaptation, must be compared in terms of their contribution to internal adaptation and group survival. Two essential evolutionary questions then emerge: (1) What is the process involved in the spread or replacement of cultural traits? (Internal adaptation.) (2) Which traits contribute to an increase in carrying capacity and death control, and how do they do this? (External adaptation.) The effectiveness of adaptive traits must be measured in relation to increases in carrying capacity and concomitant increases in population.

Evolution is a process through which systems develop and are modified in relation to specific environmental backgrounds. All the theory requires is that there be mechanisms of variation (producing new variables) and mechanisms of continuity (preserving maximization) present in these systems and that these systems be subject to environmental selection. Maximization is measured in terms of the effectiveness of self-regulation and ensuing population success. There is no requirement that the mechanisms of variation and continuity be specifically biological in nature, as long as they operate within biological systems, and human populations must be taken as one type of biological system. If the theory of evolution is seen as a theory about process, the distinctions between so-called biological and cultural evolution disappear. The mechanisms which produce or change culture traits are a subtype of general evolutionary mechanism. Furthermore, in any adaptive system cultural and biological factors may each modify behavior, and each other, and these modifications may then affect the state of the behavioral system or act to transform it into another system.[4]

[4] Changes in the state of a system refer to homeostatic responses in which the system adjusts to variations in the environmental field. System transformations refer to the transgenerational emergence of new systems, some of which may be better adapted than any previous system.

While in the broad sense the evolutionary process is the same for all species, the operating rules for those mechanisms which produce cultural traits are not the same as those which produce biologically determined somatic or behavioral traits. This is why some of the analogies between biological and cultural evolution fail. To call the process of innovation in culture a mutation, for example, is to depart from the logical model of evolution. Mutations involve somatic changes, and become fixed in a population only through genetic transmission. Reference to the process of diffusion as a kind of gene flow is unjustified for the same reasons. Nor is it correct to draw analogies between species on the one hand and cultures on the other. Species are biologically defined closed units; cultures certainly are not. Furthermore, in Simpson's (1961) terms, culture is a species' specific adaptation of man.

In sum, it is the subject matter as well as the process of adaptation, and not the mechanisms of change, which should be seen as the same for somatic and cultural evolution. If one considers human populations as the subject matter for research rather than "Cultures," then these units may be treated equally well as behavioral or physical entities. If the biological model is adhered to, we shall be forced to recognize the connections which must exist between genetic and extragenetic events. We shall also come to see that the thorough study of human adaptation is essentially a biological problem involving, in part, a very important series of nongenetic processes.

It must be made clear that I am not suggesting in any way that genes determine cultures. It is only the capacity for culture that is genetic, and this capacity is panhuman. In addition it is well known that the direction of culture change as well as the complexity of any particular human behavioral system are generally independent of any particular gene pool. The existence of human "behavioral" genes is certainly not to be disputed, however; the human species is not exempt from partial genetic control over behavior. It is also probable that differences in the frequency of certain "behavioral" genes exist among human populations. But such variations are not likely to produce consistent behavioral differences because of what must be the strong effect of culture on the penetrance of such genes. The most deterministic thing about the human behavioral genetic system is bound to be its openness. There is no doubt that it allows for a tremendous amount of nongenetic coding.

The point to be made here is that cultural adaptation is as much a biological process as is genetic adaptation, and that there is bound to be some overlap between genetic and nongenetic events within the life stream of a population. Thus the student of human evolution must concern himself with genetic and nongenetic adaptation as well as with the dichotomy between internal and external adaptation. These factors may be combined in a fourfold table, which will, I hope, serve to clarify the relationships obtaining among them.

Given a population system, a change in any one of the adaptive modes (a cell in the table) may have an effect on any other. Changes in environmental parameters may also alter selection pressures on any or all of these adaptive modes.

	Genetic	Nongenetic
Internal Adaptation	physiological homeostatic systems	cultural homeostatic systems
External Adaptation	physiological environmental adaptation	cultural environmental adaptation

The interaction patterns which obtain between these modes and the environment should be a major concern of anthropological analysis. For it is only through such an analysis that we shall come to understand that complex process which constitutes human evolution. Of all the disciplines concerned with human behavior, anthropology is best suited for such a task. But this will remain true only if the traditional four-field approach of American anthropology is maintained.

The epidemiological patterns which vary from population to population provide interesting material for the analysis of the adaptive process. In general, the incidence of disease is related to genetic and nongenetic factors. Any change in a behavioral system is likely to have medical consequences, some of which will produce changes in the genetic system. On the other hand, disease-induced changes in the genetic structure can affect the behavioral system. Such effects may be the result of population restructuring

49

or the emergence of new immunological patterns which alter the possibilities for niche exploitation. In addition, induced or natural alterations in the environmental field provide new selective pressures relating to health and disease which must be met through a combination of somatic and nonsomatic adaptations.

One of the most interesting, if still somewhat controversial, examples of the interaction between infectious disease, genetic change, and behavior is that documented by Livingstone (1958). This concerns the relationship between a culturally produced expansion of the habitat for the mosquito carrier of falciparum malaria and an increase in the frequency of the recessive gene for sickle cell anemia. The rise in gene frequency is related to a hypothetical adaptive polymorphism in which heterozygote carriers for the sickle cell gene are immune to falciparum malaria. Wiesenfeld (1967) has recently expanded the discussion of this interaction by suggesting that a feedback relationship exists between genetic change and behavior, which can be used to explain the expansion of agriculture and agricultural peoples in West Africa:

In the case of an intensely malarious environment created by a new agricultural situation, the viability of the normal individual is reduced and there is selection for the individual with the sickle-cell trait; this means that the nature of the gene-pool of the population will change through time. This biological change helps to maintain the cultural change causing the new cellular environmental change, and the biological change may allow further development of the cultural adaptation, which in turn increases the selective pressure to maintain the biological change. In this way it is possible to see human biology and culture interacting and differentiating together in a stepwise fashion. If valid, the hypothesis developed here serves to demonstrate the important role that disease may have in human evolution." (Wiesenfeld 1967:1139)

For clarification let me say that the hypothesis developed serves to demonstrate the important role that disease may have in human evolution *and* culture change, that is, behavioral evolution as well.

CHAPTER 3

THE ECOLOGY OF HUMAN DISEASE

INFECTIOUS DISEASE

Confrontation between man and his microscopic parasites are numerous and varied. These confrontations affect the process by which behavioral choices are sorted out in a developing sociocultural system. Thus they become factors in the overall process of adaptation. In this section I shall outline those cultural and biological factors which are of major importance to epidemiological patterns.

Among the biological characteristics to be outlined here, some are concerned with the properties of the host, others with properties of the parasites themselves. While these characteristics are discussed separately, I must emphasize that specific disease patterns depend upon the combined effects of these characteristics and the cultural practices which may be related to them.

SIZE, DENSITY, AND MOVEMENT OF HUMAN POPULATIONS

Epidemics like people. There are certain optimal numbers which make a population more susceptible to the rapid spread of epidemic disease. While these optimums vary according to specific diseases, in general the higher the population density the greater the chance that microorganisms will make a successful transfer from host to host. This situation is true for both contagious and noncontagious infectious disease. In the latter case the size of the vector and reservoir populations is also important. In general pest populations vary directly with size of the human populations within which they are imbedded.

Outbreaks of certain epidemic diseases may be related to Malthusian controls. According to recent students of disease history the great plagues of Europe appear to be associated with high population densities as well as with large overall populations in relation to per capita production. According to Roberts (1966):

. . . England was at that time much more densely populated than is usually thought. Since the time of the Dooms-day Book in 1086 the population seems to have trebled, from 1.1 million to 3.5 million (Russell 1948, p. 280). In the absence of technical advances, or import of foodstuffs, this greatly increased population could only be fed by a commensurate increase in the area of cultivated land. The enclosure of waste land and the settlement of new villages in the thirteenth century shows that this indeed was done on a large scale. The disproportionate increase in rents, however, equally shows that there was still not enough land and the inevitable Malthusian checks then came into operation . . .
. . . It was only the social and economic crisis of the 1340s, however, which seems to have created the necessary conditions—rats brought into closer contact with man

in the search for food after bad harvests, movement of populations after famine and epidemics, overcrowding perhaps in certain favoured areas and a general decline in health and resistance to disease." (Roberts 1966:102)

In addition to population size, the arrangement of living space plays an important role in the spread or containment of disease. Thus the type and arrangements of houses, the number of rooms per dwelling, and the number of occupants per room all contribute to epidemiological patterns.

Social isolation of various subgroups is also important to disease ecology. A rigid caste system with minimal social and physical contact between groups may affect epidemic routes in a community for at least some diseases. Class differentiation may also have its effects on the disease pattern. To quote Roberts again:

By the time of the Great Plague . . . the population of London had risen from about 90,000 to about 460,000 (Brett-James 1935, pp. 496-503). This great increase had led to severe overcrowding in a ring of out-parishes and Liberties which stretched around the city of London in a semi-circle from Holborn to Stepney; and it was from these slums that plague periodically made its forays into the City itself. . . .

As usually happened, all who could afford to do so left London in 1665; and as the number of plague deaths rose in the hot weather of June and July, so the flight from London grew greater . . . .

. . . Thus the City which had about half of London's total population suffered only one-seventh of the deaths (Bell 1924, pp. 123, 273). The Liberties of the City and the outparishes, on the other hand, became even more crowded than usual because many of the lower classes who normally lived and worked in the City now found themselves without employment or their customary poor-relief, and so were forced into these poorer suburbs (Bell 1924:68, 91). Here there was no organization or authority to deal with the crisis. . . . (Roberts 1966:104)

The plot of Ben Jonson's *The Alchemist*, set in London during the plague years, is based partially on the flight of the rich. The play's action centers around the servants of a wealthy man who has deserted his house during the epidemic.

Population movement is another important variable. Nomads tend to leave their waste products behind them, while sedentary people live in more or less constant contact with their own refuse. Where and how they dispose of this refuse are epidemiological factors. The larger a population becomes in relation to a specific area the greater the problems of disposal of wastes.

Nomadic populations may also carry certain diseases over long distances. Markets are a good place for the exchange and redistribution of disease organisms as well as goods and services. Contact between different cultural groups, which is rather frequent in market societies, may bring about cross infection.

Visiting patterns within and between villages of the same ethnic group also affect epidemiological patterns. Area-wide attendance at funerals and the length of such ceremonies may influence the level and distribution of infection during epidemics.

THE ECOLOGY OF HUMAN DISEASE

THE ORGANISM'S ENVIRONMENT
OUTSIDE THE HUMAN HOST

Many organisms associated with infectious disease spend a part of their life cycle outside the human host. Others must be capable of surviving at least long enough for successful transfer between hosts. Parasites carried by vectors may reproduce and pass through morphological stages in an animal or insect carrier. Others are commonly found in water, still others in soil, and some are found only in human and/or animal excrement. Cultural practices which effectively separate man from the organism's extra-human environment act to control the incidence of disease in human populations. If human and animal carriers are denied access to such environments, the disease cycle may be broken. Deep latrines offer protection against many intestinal infections which are spread through contact with waste products. However, such latrines make retrieval of such material for fertilizer difficult, and they are not found where night soil is an important aspect of the agricultural system.

Care of the water supply or its location away from domestic animals and human habitation may protect it from contamination. The penning of domestic animals to prevent their feces from being spread through a habitation area, or the removal of such material, will substantially reduce the chance of transference of enzootic and epizootic diseases to man.

Certain geographic and microclimatic factors influence the viability of organisms. The parasite of yaws, for example, can survive only in warm, moist soil. The disease is limited in its distribution by noncultural climatic factors. On the other hand, many helminths which have been demonstrated to infect Eskimo populations exist only because of a warm, moist, artificial microclimate produced as a by-product of dwelling conditions.

VIABILITY OF THE ORGANISM

As a rule of thumb, disease organisms may be rated from highly viable (spore formers) to least viable (organisms of venereal disease). Organisms which spread in the air and are resistant to long desiccation are particularly difficult to eliminate from a population. Those which survive only in a liquid or semiliquid environment (food, water, feces, and other waste) may be eliminated by boiling or cooking in the case of food and water, or by burying in the case of offensive matter. Simple water storage before use may eliminate some parasites; guinea worm and schistosomiasis organisms cannot survive long periods outside the host. Personal and village hygiene levels are directly related to the spread or containment of specific diseases, and organisms of low to moderate viability are most susceptible to general hygienic measures.

MODE OF INFECTION

Organisms may gain entry to the host through the unbroken skin (schistosomiasis, ancylostomiasis), the mouth (most intestinal parasites, guinea worm, the dysenteries), the nose (viruses carried in the air, such as influenza; bacteria causing pneumonia and bronchitis), injection from vectors (encephalitis, malaria, yellow fever, plague, leishmaniasis, dengue, relapsing fever, filariasis), wounds (yaws, gangrene, tropical ulcer, tetanus), or contact with mucous membranes (venereal diseases). They may also affect the surface of the body (fungus and arthropod infections).

The avoidance of infected water sources is the only protection against schistosomiasis. Aerosol infections may be prevented by isolating the sick. Promiscuous spitting increases the probable spread of many viruses and *Mycobacterium tuberculosis*. Protection against injection depends upon an understanding of the host-vector relationship and/or practices which tend to limit the insect population. Wounds must be covered and contact between infected and normal individuals avoided. Venereal patients must be isolated or they should refrain from sexual intercourse. Polygyny, in combination with adultery and other forms of promiscuity, may increase the frequency of contact between infected and normal individuals. Fungus infections may be discouraged by avoiding contact with sick individuals, by boiling contaminated water, through frequent washing (except where the fungus is waterborne) and, in certain conditions by shaving body hair.

Certain organisms (anaerobic bacteria such as *Clostridium tetani*) are infectious only if they gain entry to the host through deep puncture wounds. The type of tools used and kind of work done by members of a population may influence the frequency of this sort of injury.

VIABILITY AND TYPE OF VECTOR
AND CARRIER

Vectors may be divided into two types: mechanical, when the disease organism is merely transported
by the vector; breeding, when the organism depends
on the vector for part of its life cycle. The range and
habitat of vectors vary considerably. Fleas and lice
live on the body of the host, but fleas jump readily
from one host to another while lice spread primarily
via shared clothing or bedding. Tailored clothing presents a better environment for lice than loose togas.
Tapa cloth, which must be replaced frequently, is the
least favorable environment for these vectors. Flies
and mosquitoes are highly mobile, but mosquitoes
prefer to fly at night, or in deep shade, while flies
prefer daylight. One rarely needs protection against
mosquitoes in the heat of day, and eating at night or
in the early morning may protect food from fly-borne
contamination. Some ticks live in the underbrush generally away from human habitation; others are domestic insects, preferring the cracks in mud walls and
house roofing to the bush. The clearing of paths
around villages is good protection against ticks of the
first type. The practice of erecting rest houses along
trails increases the possibility that domestic tick infections will spread from area to area.

Some rodents are also domestic and live in intimate
contact with man; others normally live away from
human habitation but act as disease reservoirs, sometimes passing infections to the domestic rodent population. Any practice, such as the partial conversion of
forested land into agricultural land, which increases

the possibility of contact between wild and domestic rodent strains also increases the possibility of disease transference. On the other hand, the complete elimination of wild rodent habitats also eliminates the disease reservoir population.

Even mosquitoes may be classified as wild or domestic in the sense that some breed best in and around villages in trash heaps (*Aedes* mosquitoes are good examples), while others require natural habitats (most *Anopheles* mosquitoes). The flight patterns of biting insects is also important and variable. Some have very limited flight ranges (sand flies; certain varieties of *Glossina* or tsetse flies; *Aedes* mosquitoes), while others may cover a wide area (*Culex* mosquitoes). Certain insects prefer to feed on humans; others bite a wide range of domestic and wild animals as well. When the latter is the case, it is possible that much infection is diverted to domestic animals living with man, but such animals also constitute a reservoir of infection. This is true, for example, of yellow fever, which infects monkeys as well as human beings.

The requisite habitat of insects varies according to particular stages of life cycle, for example, egg, larva, pupa, and adult. Bates (1949) lists the following important aspects of the environment: resting place, vertical stratification, light intensity, temperature requirements, moisture requirements, and activity time cycles. The importance of light intensity has been amply demonstrated in the case of *Anopheles gambiens*, which must breed in sunlit pools. Livingstone has offered the interesting hypothesis that falciparum malaria did not spread widely in West Africa until the introduction of agriculture and iron tools. The change in productive techniques had the effect of increasing the available breeding grounds for *A. gambiae*, the major carrier of falciparum malaria in the area.

Bates (1949:16) writes of vertical stratification among mosquito species: "The swarms of pest mosquitoes of the flood plains of tropical rivers are all ground pool breeders."

Bates goes on to quote Humboldt: "The good missionary, Bernardo Zea, who passes his life under the torment of mosquitoes, has constructed himself, near his church, upon a scaffolding of palm trunks, a little room in which he can breathe more freely. We mounted there in the evening by the help of a ladder, to dry out plants and to write up our journey. The missionary had noticed with exactness that insects abound mostly in the lower layer of the atmosphere, that which is near the soil, up to twelve to fifteen feet in height."

The species' specific nature of vertical stratification is illustrated in Bates (1949:17), in which the capture frequencies at different heights above the forest floor of *Anopheles gambiae* and bearing *Aedes africanus* are compared.

In addition to rodents and arthropods, important parasite-bearing organisms include mollusks and small crustacea. Snails, which carry schistosomiasis (bilharzia) and cyclops, a microscopic shrimp-like organism which carries dracunculosis (guinea worm), are limited to particular sorts of watery environments. Irrigation increases the spread of schistosoma-carrying snails, while the techniques involved in wet rice cultivation lead to frequent contact between human hosts and the parasite environment.

Wells, if they are covered, discourage guinea worm, unless infected individuals bathe their sores at the side of the well. Unfortunately, this is a common practice because the parasite produces a burning sensation at its exit site, usually the ankle. Thus guinea worm is relatively common even in those areas where water resources are scarce. Victims will seek out available water to bathe their sores. The gravid female promptly extrudes her ovipositer and deposits her eggs in the requisite environment. Step wells, common in India, are particularly dangerous watering sites because infected individuals get their feet and ankles wet as they stoop to fill their water containers.

Domestic animals may carry infections transferable to man, and provide a reservoir of disease. Among those diseases transferable to man the best-known are brucellosis (undulant fever) and bovine tuberculosis, carried by cattle; anthrax, carried by sheep, swine, and cattle; and creeping eruption (dog hookworm). Domestic animals may also carry insect vectors which may attack human hosts. Sheep ticks, which carry spotted fever, are particularly dangerous. Domestic animal populations always increase the possibility of parasitic contamination of the human population. When they are harbored within a habitation area the risk is increased.

INCUBATION PERIOD

The incubation period, which is that period of time between contact with the agent and the development of symptoms, varies considerably. Where incubation periods are short and the disease severe, plague for example, nomadic populations or traveling merchants are less likely to spread a disease than when incubation periods are long and the host has time to cover considerable distances before symptoms appear.

SYMPTOMS AND PRODROMAL SYMPTOMS

The recognition of symptoms produces an interesting intersection between biological and cultural factors. The type of category system developed by a people may affect their ability to recognize disease and to isolate people before contagion becomes a serious problem. Where prodromal symptoms are recognized speedy isolation may be particularly effective. Proper identification of specific conditions also increases the possibility of producing effective cures.

Certain diseases have more discrete symptomologies than others. Measles, chickenpox, and smallpox may be confused in some cultures and distinguished in others. The various forms of leprosy, yaws, and syphilis may be recognized as manifestations of these same three diseases, or each symptom category may be used to tag a separate, ethnically defined illness. Symptoms may be seen as discrete units (headache unrelated to fever, unrelated to rash), or they may be combined to describe a specific condition. The ability to recognize symptoms is important in the effective treatment of disease, and effective treatment in turn influences not only the rates of a particular treated condition but also overall health within any given population. Treatment of one condition may act as

63

an effective barrier against one or more other conditions.

I will have much more to say about native systems of diagnosis and treatment in Chapter 6.

NONGENETIC FACTORS IN RESISTANCE

Even where the virility of the parasite is constant, the receptivity of the host may vary. Diet, work loads, sleep, exposure, and other forms of stress are all factors which affect resistance. Most of these factors are related to the behavioral system, but sex, age, and previous medical history may also play a role in resistance.

IMMUNITY

The incidence and severity of disease may also depend upon the availability of susceptibles within a population. Epidemics of such diseases as measles cycle predictably through time, striking only when a new generation of nonimmunes takes its place in the community. A correlation between the ceremonial calendar and this type of cycling might spread disease through a gathering of celebrants. It might be interesting to look at the incidence of epidemics in societies which practice age grade ceremonies involving intervillage and interregional visiting.

Immunity is, of course, either inherited, congenital, or acquired. Acquired immunity occurs when an individual has had a disease episode and recovered, or has been immunized artificially, but the disease may have produced squelae which have significant effects on the subsequent disease history of the individual. Inherited immunity, known as genetic resistance, which results from genetic structuring might have its own side effects through the plieotropic action of the gene or genes involved. Thus individuals heterozygous for the sickle cell gene are resistant to malaria, but the high frequency of the gene in the population produces a high frequency of the homozygous individuals with the fatal disease sickle cell anemia.

All types of immunity may be either partial or total. Partial immunity means, of course, that individuals can, in fact, become infected with a particular disease but that the severity of the attack is reduced.

THE EXISTENCE OF HUMAN CARRIERS

The occupational role of human carriers in disease is well known in our culture from such famous cases as Typhoid Mary, who spread disease from the kitchens in which she worked. Other diseases such as amoebic dysentery and hepatitis can also be spread by carriers. Little is known about the role of such individuals in other cultures. Are they recognized? Do certain occupations make individuals prone to such diseases? What is the strategic position of carriers in various societies? An investigation of the role of carriers in societies stratified according to castes, professions, or social classes might provide interesting data for the field of epidemiology.

Any epidemiological study must take account of the permutations and of the combinations resulting from these various biological and cultural factors acting together. To take one example: plague is caused by the bacterium *Pasteurella pestis*. The organism has low resistance outside the host. It is carried by rat fleas and does not usually affect humans until the rat population has been reduced to the point where it is not sufficient to sustain the flea population. It persists in endemic form in wild rodents (sylvatic plague). From time to time this form transfers to domestic rats. The disease has a short incubation period, a high mortality rate when untreated, rather obvious symptoms, and in its bubonic form is not transmitted from man to man directly. The rat population varies according to the type and duration of human habitation. This applies not only to the size of the rat population but also to the variety of rat which is most frequent.

Any effect which a human population has upon the wild rodent reservoir population may be related to an initial transfer of plague vectors to domestic rats. The clearing of new land may bring wild and domestic rodent populations into closer contact, while the elimination of all uncultivated land may reduce the wild rodent population to the point where it ceases to exist as a reservoir. The hunting of wild rodents for skins or food may produce an occasional case of plague but is unlikely to produce an epidemic.

The high mortality rates and short incubation period of the disease means that single infected populations would be unlikely to spread the plague over long distances through population movement, although it could be transferred rapidly from community to community through a series of short trips stimulated by an epidemic. Rat migrations are known to have transferred the disease over long as well as short distances. Health measures which protect against the immigration of foreign rats are an effective barrier to the spread of the bubonic form of plague. Isolation of the sick has little effect on the incidence of plague, and most hygienic measures offer small protection against epidemics once they have begun. Hygiene practices must be directed specifically to the elimination of rats, particularly before epidemics, and fleas.

The same disease in its pneumonic form, however, presents an entirely different epidemiological picture, since the rat-flea vectors are eliminated from the disease cycle. Pneumonic plague usually develops during an epidemic of the bubonic form and passes rapidly from host to host through direct contact. Total isolation of infected persons then becomes necessary.

A list of the behavioral factors which influence infectious disease patterns could be expanded almost indefinitely. The purpose here has been to illustrate the most important kinds of relationships which exist between behavior and certain biological characteristics of parasites and their hosts. The interaction of these variables has its effect on the total epidemiological pattern of a population, and this in turn has its effect on the behavioral system and the physical structure of the population. The cyclical effect of behavior on disease and disease on behavior must play an important role in the direction of culture change and adaptation, yet almost nothing is known of this phenomenon among non-Western populations.

NUTRITION

Infectious diseases are not the only frequently encountered pathologies. Severe nutritional disorders are common throughout the world. These disorders may be the result of multiple deficiencies or a simple dietary shortage of a single essential nutrient.

Nutritional requirements may be broken down into a few convenient categories: carbohydrates, lipids, amino acids (injested as proteins), vitamins, minerals, and water. Deficiencies in each of these categories have important consequences for health. Particular disease syndromes may be attributed to dietary deficiencies, and there is considerable evidence that malnutrition has a general effect on the overall performance level of the individual, particularly in the area of disease resistance. Detailed discussions of these deficiency diseases may be found in most medical books and in the particularly useful volume published by the Heinz Company, *The Heinz Handbook of Nutrition*. I shall limit my discussion here to dietary choice, differential caloric requirements, and the anthropological implications of malnutrition, particularly in the area of low protein intake.

While undernutrition is common in some parts of the world, by far the greater problem is malnutrition, the improper intake of necessary elements in the diet. The single most widespread deficiency disease is protein malnutrition.

The conversion of environmentally produced nutrients into the specific chemical requirements of a species is a highly involved process. Mechanisms which reduce or economize on the complexity of this operation have evolved in all living systems. Thus for example, certain genes are activated only in the presence of particular substrates; others are deactivated when the reaction end products reach functional levels. Certain lower organisms such as viruses, bacteria, and even simple multicellular forms are capable of synthesizing most metabolic products. Plants, through the process of photosynthesis, produce complex molecules from water, sunlight, and minerals. In many cases the synthesizing capabilities of the cell are restricted, and complex molecules taken from the external environment become necessary for the continuance of the life process.

Higher animals must take in not only simple inorganic chemicals but complex organic molecules as well. Among mammals, herbivores are capable of synthesizing many amino acids, but carnivores have partially lost this ability. The metabolic systems of these animals are geared to breaking down complex protein molecules into basic amino acids and building them up again to fit the specific requirement of the system. It is no paradox that a loss of basic synthesizing capability provides a twofold gain for such organisms. First of all it allows them to cut down on a wide variety of superfluous chemical reactions in cells which are already enormously busy, and, second, it allows these organisms, which are behaviorally capable of obtaining required nutrients from their environment, to build chemical structures tailored to their more complex morphological and physiological systems.

It is obvious from both his morphology and his chemical system that man was born to be a meat eater. The human physiological system, capable as it is, is able to synthesize only some amino acids and vitamin D. Other essential amino acids must be absorbed from meat or plant food, but a vegetarian diet is unlikely to provide these food elements unless it is carefully planned. This kind of metabolic system was completely congruent with human behavior until the advent of the neolithic revolution, the period of plant domestication. The shift from a primarily meat diet to one based more or less on agricultural products created dietary problems in many regions of the world. The gain in stability of production and in output was enormous.

Since caloric requirements go well beyond the small amount of protein necessary for the maintenance of health, agricultural technologies could support much larger populations. Health could be maintained through the eating of meat harvested from hunting and/or killing of domestic animals. In addition, in the cereal-growing regions of the world protein malnutrition and vitamin deficiencies were rare because unrefined grain is quite high in most of the necessary nutrients. But in tropical areas, particularly in those geographic zones in which grain crops do poorly and where the major domesticates are root crops such as the yam, sweet potato, manioc, and taro, protein scarcity becomes a severe problem. Populations lacking domestic animals for one reason or another must rely on hunting to fulfill protein requirements. A growing and stable population, increased in part because of agriculture, would rapidly deplete the natural game supply and create new nutritional problems.

In most cases it is likely that such populations

would be checked in part by Malthusian controls with protein or, more correctly, certain essential amino acids as the limiting factors. Infectious disease may have also played a significant part in the checking of population growth, particularly in stable, compact agricultural communities. Today the introduction of Western medicine in such regions puts strains on the entire population and increases the protein deficit. Malnourished individuals who might otherwise succumb to disease survive with possible damaging consequences for the entire population (see Cravioto et al. 1966).

Protein requirements are highest in children. Protein malnutrition in the first months of life may be particularly damaging to the developing nervous system. Populations in regions with an inadequate protein supply must develop some kind of behavioral adaptation to this situation or face severe difficulties. One possible adaptation has been the development of a series of behaviors which favor long nursing periods for infants. John Whiting (1964) has suggested that long postpartum taboos on sexual relations, or in tropical South America abortions, are linked to late weaning as a protective device for the mother's milk. Whiting assumes that a pregnant woman's milk is somehow reduced in nutritional quality.

There is little evidence at the present time to either support or reject this hypothesis, but it stands to reason that in populations with substandard diets the mother's system is under enough stress without the added burden of producing milk and nourishing a growing fetus at the same time. Females are structured so that even when their nutritional status is

71

poor they continue to produce good quality milk, at great expense to their own health. But there must be limits and Whiting's hypothesis is certainly a reasonable one.

One of his interesting findings is a correlation between long postpartum taboos, or the custom of widespread abortions, for nursing mothers among populations dependent for most of their caloric requirements on root crops. These areas include Tropical Africa, Tropical South America, South Asia, and the Pacific. Severe protein malnutrition (kwashiorkor), which is a constant threat to children in these populations, may well be reduced in overall incidence by customs which maintain long nursing periods, although such customs may become inefficient with further population growth and greater restrictions on protein intake.

Recently Cravioto et al. (1966) studied the effects of malnutrition, particularly protein deficiency, on the mental performance of children in Guatemala. Dividing their peasant populations into four groups, on the basis of height, they tested the mental performance of the tallest and shortest quartiles. The assumption here was that the shortest reflected an episode of malnutrition during the early developmental process and that the tallest children represented the best nourished subgroup in the population. There was a strong correlation between height and test performance. The possibility that differences in height were based on genetic factors alone, and that these might somehow be correlated with mental performance, was accounted for by taking a generally better nourished urban population as a control. In the urban group height was not found to be related to performance on the same tests. Furthermore, height in the urban group was significantly related to parental height, while in the rural group it was not. The only significant correlation between parents and children in the rural group was the educational level of the mother. Poorer educated mothers were highly correlated with short children (also poor performers). Better educated mothers had taller children who performed better in the mental tests.

The authors concluded that those mothers with poorer educational standards were more likely to practice poor nutrition in their households, and thus affect the physiological functioning and morphological growth of their offspring. The authors raised the important and neglected problem of the cyclical effect produced by the survival of mentally retarded individuals who might otherwise succumb to disease but survive to produce new generations of further damaged children. In general this is the outcome of public health measures which consider only physical health.

Taken together the Whiting and Cravioto studies appear to contradict each other. Whiting suggests that a widespread behavioral adjustment has at least partially overcome a nutritional problem, while the Cravioto study suggests that the diet of uneducated peasants is maladaptive. I should like to offer two hypothetical explanations for this apparent contradiction. In the first place "primitive" populations have had longer to adjust to conditions than Latin American peasants whose culture is, at least in part, a European transplant. Peasant groups function within behavioral systems, which some anthropologists have referred to as part cultures. Such behavioral systems are the outcome of combinations of European and native practices.

In the second place the partial dependence of peasant populations on an external behavioral system and their subjugation to an economic system over which they have no control make them more vulnerable to the fixation of practices which may in fact be maladaptive in terms of the local environment. In addition the possibility should not be overlooked that the larger system of which peasant populations are only a part might prove to be sociologically and biologically viable in spite of any esthetic or humanitarian revulsion which the system may engender. (A high death rate among peasant children may be a factor in keeping population within the carrying capacity of the land.) This is not to say that if systems, when examined in their larger framework, appear to be more adaptive or functional than a traditional examination might reveal they are to be condoned as morally right. Certainly our ethic does not derive from biological considerations alone. Furthermore, there is more than one way to meet the biological requirements of populations. Once an ethic has been decided upon and this is a problem of cultural relativity, "more ethical" systems can be substituted for "less ethical ones." The problem is of course that lack of a sensible overview of such problems can lead to ethical mismanagement and biological destruction of the population at the same time.

A little explored area of nutritional ecology is the possible relationship between the carrying capacity of the environment and body mass. One possible biological adaptation to reduced availability of both calories and protein is a reduction in size with a concomitant reduction of individual requirements. One of my students, Mrs. Georgeda Bick, has found a high correlation between nutritional status and body size in New Guinea. This is not a new idea. Since the war, for example, the average height of Japanese has increased with positive dietary changes. It is also well known that the American population has been growing taller each generation for the past several generations. What is new in Mrs. Bick's study is her hypothesis that such a relationship may be biologically adaptive in relating the average size of an individual within a population to its natural environment and mode of subsistence. It is possible that various human populations which have persisted in nutritionally deprived areas have made some genetic and/or physiological adjustive responses to such deprivation.

It is well known that certain populations like the Bemba of East Africa go through long periods of what are considered to be substandard caloric intake during their yearly cycles. Nonetheless they survive. Too little is known about variations in dietary requirements in different populations existing under different types of nutritional stress, and nothing at all is known about the type of response such stress might engender. In what cases, if any, does it depend upon a genetic base, and what role does physiological adaptation based on plasticity play in such adjustments?

There is also a behavioral side to this question.

Dubos (1965) cites a study of protein intake and starvation in pig populations. In the experimental group pigs were fed on a high protein diet prior to starvation. The control group subsisted on a normal protein intake. During the test period both groups were restricted to water. The experimental group showed evidence of starvation considerably earlier than the control population. Its nitrogen loss was also much higher. The experiment suggests that overfeeding with protein is actually detrimental if such a diet is followed by starvation. Pig physiology is amazingly similar to that of humans, and there is a strong possibility that the same response would be found in humans as well. It may be that diets which are low but still adequate in some nutrients may be adaptive for those populations which experience periods of complete deprivation for part of the year.

On the other hand, there appears to be some relationship between protein intake and resistance to infectious disease. Antibody production is related to protein intake because the basic building blocks of antibody molecules are the essential amino acids. Nevertheless it has been difficult to demonstrate direct relationships between diet and resistance to specific diseases. The possibility that substances found in certain foods in the diet of specific human populations contribute to disease resistance should certainly be investigated.

The habit of many primitive peoples of eating considerably more protein during times of stress (funerals, war parties, etc.) may be related to an adaptation in which antibody production is mobilized in times of greatest need and stress. Roy Rappaport

(1968) has suggested such an adaptive mechanism for the Maring of New Guinea.

Even rather gross behavioral configurations may be related to the solution of what are basically nutritional problems. Sahlins (1968) has pointed out that typical hunting and gathering populations solved their subsistence needs rather well, often with a minimum of exertion. He argues that in preagricultural times many hunting and gathering groups were distributed in game-rich environments. The groups which we see today are remnants of populations which have been pushed into less favorable habitats by more numerous and better organized neolithic (agricultural) peoples.

Early reports of hunting populations suggest that leisure time, at least for men, exceeded time spent in food-seeking activities. Work patterns found among many hunters and gatherers even today tend to confirm this suggestion. It appears that females spend a much greater time in gathering than the men do in hunting. I would link this behavior to nutritional problems by offering the hypothesis that such patterns of work distribution represent a highly adaptive form of behavior in relation to protein-calorie requirements. Caloric requirements are quite high, at least 3,000 calories per day for active people, although the figure varies according to size as well as activity. Protein requirements are quite low, about 45 grams per day. Protein sources include both plant and animal foods, but it is important to note that in general plant protein lacks one or another of the essential amino acids, all of which are found in meat. Therefore meat in the diet is the only simple way to assure the full compliment of these essential elements.

In most hunting and gathering societies, as well as in many simple agricultural groups, those individuals responsible for providing overall caloric needs are the women. Their task includes the provision of surplus calories for the energy output required in hunting. Hunters, who for good biological reasons are men, invest these calories in the protein quest. The caloric output from the products of hunting may frequently fall below the investment, but an essential element is added to the diet. Obviously, if a group is to survive, the caloric deficit produced by hunting must be less than the surplus provided by gathering. Hunters must maximize their behavioral strategies so that the calorie deficit produced through hunting is less than or (minimally) equal to the surplus provided by gathering. Put another way, hunters should hunt enough to meet amino acid requirements but not so much that they strain the overall caloric supply. Restrictions on hunting also serve to conserve game for peoples who have no storage facilities and must depend on a constant renewal of the local fauna.

Such an adaptive pattern need not be consciously derived. Groups that strain their resources cannot survive caloric deficit. They must either change their behavior or die out. Eskimos are surely an exception to the pattern described. Men provide the major source of both calories and protein, but this is due to the exigencies of a particular environmental setting. Females in Eskimo culture may be more sedentary than the men and thus act as the calorie conservers in the population. Plains Indian buffalo hunters provided another exceptional case. The major calorie expenditure, however, was produced by horses rather than men. Since these animals could feed on readily available plant resources, they acted as mechanism for the conversion of plant energy (of a type which humans cannot use directly) into high-grade protein and calories for human consumption.

STRESS

The concept of stress as a general medical phenomenon is closely tied to the name of Hans Selye, who is responsible for the major synthesizing work in this area. Early in his career Selye noticed that the body is responsive to a wide range of diseases according to a general response pattern, which he named the General Adaptation Syndrome (GAS). This response pattern develops as the body mobilizes its forces against a wide range of irritating agents from the invasion of parasites to purely emotional interactions. The symptoms of this response include: (1) enlargement of the adrenal cortex; (2) atrophy of the thymus, spleen, and lymph nodes; (3) bleeding deep ulcers.

Selye demonstrated that tissues which were more directly involved in the stressful situation, those, for example, which were at the site of irritation, developed what he calls the Local Adaptation Syndrome (LAS). According to Selye, "the LAS and the GAS are closely coordinated. Chemical alarm signals are sent out by directly stressed tissue, from the LAS area to the centers of coordination in the nervous system and to endocrine glands, especially the *pituitary* and the *adrenals*, which produce *adaptive hormones*, to combat wear and tear on the body. Thus the generalized response (GAS) acts back upon the LAS region." (Selye 1956:47)

Some of the responses outlined by Selye might appear to be detrimental to the system, and, in fact, the stress reaction is often the major producer of characteristic disease symptoms. This paradox can be explained on two separate grounds. First, the adaptive response comes in three stages: (1) the alarm reaction; (2) the stage of resistance; and (3) the stage of exhaustion. If the stress upon the organism is too great, the response fails to produce effective results (restoration of homeostasis), and the inevitable result is death. In the second place, Selye points out that, in many cases of disease, inflammation at the site serves the purpose of limiting and isolating the infective agent within the system so that it may be more effectively combatted. It is also a feature of the response syndrome that the body is capable of producing irritation-reducing substances under certain circumstances.

The adaptive hormones fall into two groups: the anti-inflammatory hormones (ACTH, cortisone, COL) which inhibit excessive defensive reactions, and the proinflammatory hormones (STH, aldosterone, DOC) which stimulate them. The effects of all these substances can be modified or conditioned by other hormones (adrenalins or thyroid hormone), nervous reactions, diet, heredity and the tissue memories of previous exposures to stress. Derailments of this GAS-mechanism produce wear-and-tear diseases, that is, *diseases of adaptation*. In a nutshell, the response to stress has a tripartite mechanism, consisting of: (1) the direct effect of the stressor on the body; (2) internal responses which stimulate tissue-defense; and (3) internal responses which stimulate tissue-surrendered by inhibiting defense. *Resistance and adaptation depend on a proper balance of these three factors.* (Selye 1956:47)

There are instances in which incompatible reactions occur within the system. One of these is the result of psychological stress occurring concurrently with physiological disease. Inflammation resulting from parasitic or mechanically induced stress may under certain conditions, such as anxiety, be reduced through the secretion of anti-inflammatory hormones. The overall result is a worsening of the original condition. Selye describes an experimental study of this particular syndrome:

I took some rats and made air sacks on their backs in the usual manner but without introducing an irritant. Immediately after this I injected 5 cc of fresh gastric juice. The adjacent tissues of the skin were digested within a few hours . . . then I made a similar air sac but injected some croton oil [an irritant] into it, so as to transform them into an inflammatory barricade before introducing the gastric juice into the cavity. Now no digestion of the adjacent tissue occurred. An inflammatory barricade, such as always paves the crater of gastric ulcers, is in itself adequate protection against digestion under normal conditions.

Next I repeated the same experiment and then exposed the animals to stress [immobilization]. This produced a perforating peptic ulcer on the back of the rat. During stress, presumably due to the secretion of anti-inflammatory hormones, the barricade became so weakened that the gastric juice digested it easily. Apparently in man chronic gastric ulcers, which normally are well under

81

control, also perforate during stress, because an excess of anti-inflammatory stimuli break down the resistance of the barricade. (Selye 1956:180)

Such an incompatible reaction is apparently also the cause of distress when ACTH and cortisone are used for an inflammatory disease in patients who are suffering from gastrointestinal ulcers at the same time. Cortisone or ACTH therapy in these cases makes the ulcers worse and may even produce them if a latent tendency was present prior to therapy.

While psychological stress may occur in all animals, man is a particularly susceptible species. This is because purely symbolic factors such as fear of ghosts or demons may provoke strong anxiety. In addition, many humans are subject to such phenomena as guilt feelings, repressed emotions, and strong competitive feelings, all of which are capable of producing physiological symptoms. Psychosomatic disease depends largely on the psychological environment of the individual, who in turn is conditioned by the behavioral system. The degree and type of mental illness which may occur in a particular individual may depend in part upon the kind of psychological stress present. Schizophrenia, which many theorists now believe to have a strong genetic element in its etiology (Huxley et al. 1964), is also a disease of stress as are other psychoses and neuroses. The situation is complicated, however, by the possibility that potential schizophrenics are more highly resistant to physical stress than normal people, and by the fact that physiological defense reactions to mild stress in

82

one area (cold, shock, disease, etc.) might confer relative immunity to other forms of stress. Very little experimentation has been carried out on this problem, and such work is made difficult by the problems of control, particularly when it is almost impossible (except in the case of identical twins) to hold genetic factors constant. At any rate, the genetic and environmental elements in stress reactions probably interact in a complicated way to produce a wide range of phenotypes determined by even a wider range of genotypic and environmental interactions.

While Selye's point that stress reactions are a general class of response to threats to the integrity of the organismic system is well taken, studies of human stress which consider cultural and environmental elements must be related to interactions based on specific stressors. Thus it becomes imperative to study such problems as cold stress, high altitude stress, heat stress, and so on, and to consider these in terms of genetic adjustment, physiological plasticity, environmental factors, cultural regulators, and interaction with other physiological activity. Many interesting studies of climatic stress have already been carried out (see Baker 1963), and many more are likely to result from the International Biological Program, particularly the Human Adaptability projects (see Baker and Weiner 1966).

Nutritional stress is also an important research area. Scrimshaw (1963) has pointed out that nutritional requirements may vary from population to population and also vary as conditions change. He has also suggested that physical stress itself may interact strongly with nutritional balance. Again, such studies must consider both genetic and physiological adaptation as factors in the development of differential reactions to the nutritional base.

One of the most problematical areas of stress research is concerned with crowding. Laboratory experiments with rodent populations and certain insect species have demonstrated that overcrowding produces a lowering of fertility which is related to both physiological (particularly hormone) responses and to changes in behavior (see Thiessen 1964). Unfortunately, field experimentation tends to cast doubt upon the experimental evidence. Natural populations do indeed appear to be regulated as to size in ways which perhaps are non-Malthusian, but the responses which occur in the laboratory are not replicated in the field. When we turn to human populations the problem becomes even more complicated.

Crowding may be a relative phenomenon for man, highly dependent as he is upon symbolic configurations and experience. One of my friends from Calcutta, for example, thinks of New York as an empty city, while to a New Hampshire or Vermont farmer it may appear to be crowded and stressful. There is no evidence that crowding in human populations has any effect on population increase except for such Malthusian factors as disease and starvation, and such conscious controls as increased use of contraceptive devices. In addition we do not know what effect, if any, a television set in every room turned on for most of the day has on subjects living in rural low-density areas. Might such exposure be equivalent to crowding?

The human species is young and still spreading

into its adaptive niche. The usual response to crowding, except in the urban environment, has been dispersal to new land. Internal biological control mechanisms have yet to be demonstrated. If they exist, they would have important implications for human ecological research, since they would have to be considered in calculations of adaptation to specific environments at specific levels of carrying capacity.

CHAPTER 4

ADAPTATION TO DISEASE

Evolution may be considered a game in which one player is a population and the second player is the environment including other populations. The adaptive process begins with random moves which produce variations in structure. From the point of view of the population, somatic evolution depends on mutations and recombinations of genetic material. Cultural evolution depends on other mechanisms of variation. Winning moves allow populations to extract energy from the environment, which is converted into increased fertility. Although these moves originate in random fashion, as the game progresses, the selective process tends to reward moves which fit consistent strategies relative to the environment. These strategies develop according to the rules of a Markov process in which the probability of each move is determined by the previous move. If the game progresses successfully for the population, there will be a tendency for the number of possible moves to become reduced. Variation is lowered.

From the point of view of the environment, winning moves reduce the extractive capacities of a population, and losing moves increase it. The "best strategy" for the environment is to fluctuate as widely and as randomly as possible. This will tend to prevent the population from developing firm commitments to a specific line of adaptation. In order to guard its winnings (a certain fertility level), a population must be able to repeat winning moves. It must produce a certain continuity from generation to generation. But in order to overcome environmental fluctuations, a population must continue to generate new moves and repeat some old, normally unsuccessful, moves. Thus a population must also maintain a certain amount of variation which continues from generation to generation. In game theory language, the population must minimax its strategy. That is, it must consider possible loss as well as possible gain when choosing a series of moves.

The number of extinct populations and species testifies to the fact that the game is not always won by living organisms. On the other hand, if one considers all life as one player, a team if you like, and the environment as the other player, then the situation looks quite different. Given time, one should expect adaptation to occur in all but the harshest environments.

Evolution in general is a slow process, partly because its rather random nature is wasteful. It usually takes many moves to produce one right move. Human behavioral adaptation (cultural evolution) is particularly successful because it is a more flexible process, capable of rapid change in both quality and direction. A good deal of the randomness of variation is absent in human behavioral adaptation. Humans consciously and continually test the environment and structure these tests through the construction of theories which may be used to account for phenomena. If these theories work well they reduce environmental ambiguity and allow for the development of successful and wide-ranging adaptive strategies.

My purpose in this chapter will be to construct a partial model for the adaptive process (the game of adaptation) in relation to disease. Given the possibility that effective means of treatment or prevention can be discovered for most diseases, a simple hypothesis may be stated concerning behavioral adaptation to disease: Behavioral adaptation should be most effective against those diseases which have been present for a long time span in a population. Conversely, behavioral barriers to disease should be least effective against those diseases which are new to a population.

Stated this way the problem appears rather trivial. But only an extremely naïve individual would be expected to accept this dual hypothesis as it stands. A long series of complicating factors must be accounted for in the differential adaptation to infectious disease. The inclusion of these factors in the model increases its value for the analysis of evolutionary change.

First of all, it must be stressed that adaptation to disease may involve two different if somewhat overlapping medical systems. These are preventive medicine, in which barriers to disease are erected, and therapy. While the same disease theory may in some instances apply to both techniques, this is often not the case. Effective preventive measures may develop either partially or totally outside ethnomedical theory. Particular pathologies may be more amenable to preventive medicine while others are most easily handled through the treatment process. Which method is most effective will in turn depend upon the available medical technology.

An analysis of behavioral evolution in relation to pathology must include consideration of a set of disease characteristics. This set relates to both the biological attributes of particular diseases and the perceptions which members of a population have of them. It is my suggestion that behavioral strategies developed in response to pathology are accelerated or delayed in part by these factors taken in combination: (1) Acute vs. chronic disease; (2) complexity of the route of infection; (3) reservoir vs. nonreservoir; (4) degree of severity; (5) endemic vs. epidemic; (6) degree of prevalence and incidence; (7) discreteness of symptomology; (8) degree of contagion.

ACUTE VS. CHRONIC

The distinction here is a difficult one to make in practice. There are, however, diseases which in general may be characterized as having a rapid course, and others which produce pathological conditions of considerable duration. If a disease is acute it may be difficult to produce either preventive measures or a cure, simply because not enough time exists for successful experimentation to take place. An individual

ADAPTATION TO DISEASE

is either dead or well before enough information can be gathered. This difficulty can be overcome if the disease is highly prevalent.

COMPLEXITY OF THE ROUTE OF INFECTION

When the mode of transmission is simple (host to host contagion, for example) it should be possible to discover effective preventive measures, such as isolation. On the other hand, when the route is complex (as through a vector), preventive measures may be more difficult both to discover and to implement. It took quite some time, for example, to prove that mosquitoes were the carriers of yellow fever, even though the experimental method was used. Even when the means of transmission was demonstrated, it was difficult to eliminate the vector.

If, however, incidence and prevalence are both low, and if the disease is acute, considerable difficulty should remain. Thus, although poliomyelitis appears to have a simple mode of transmission and is highly contagious, the mode of transmission is not yet clearly understood.

RESERVOIR VS. NONRESERVOIR

The existence of a reservoir population complicates the problem of disease control, particularly when the reservoir population is wild. Yellow fever persists as a health problem because forest monkeys in both Africa and South America represent a continuing endemic focus for the disease. Plague remains a con-

90

stant threat in the United States in spite of a high level of preventive medicine and treatment because an endemic focus of the disease persists among wild rodents in the Southwestern States.

DEGREE OF SEVERITY

When a disease is severe the associated anxiety should be higher than if the condition is merely annoying. The severity of disease depends on both inherent biological characteristics of the organism and the relative resistance of the host population. In addition severity is a subjective concept which depends upon the perception of disease prevalent within the cultural system of a particular population.

ENDEMIC VS. EPIDEMIC

If a disease is endemic in a population, it is present, at least at a low level, most if not all of the time. Some conditions are endemic and common. Epidemics represent rapid and short-lasting visitations of disease. An endemic disease provides the time element necessary for experimentation. Infrequent and extremely rapid epidemics of acute diseases should be extremely difficult to deal with.

DEGREE OF PREVALENCE AND INCIDENCE

Some diseases are extremely rare either in endemic or epidemic form; others are quite common. The relative frequency of disease in terms of both incidence and prevalence could be scaled for particular populations. Rare diseases represent poor empirical conditions.

DISCRETENESS OF SYMPTOMOLOGY

Certain diseases are marked by particularly clear symptomologies, which are difficult to confuse with any other pathology. Others are quite difficult to diagnose even within the Western medical system. The relative ease with which a particular condition can be spotted depends, of course, upon the culturally determined disease theory of the local population. Category systems vary, and some are more likely to produce a high degree of empirical accuracy than others. This is an extremely important problem for medical anthropology, and I shall deal with it at greater length in the chapter on folk medical systems.

DEGREE OF CONTAGION

The more contagious a disease, the more likely the discovery of the infective route. On the other hand, a highly contagious pathology may be more difficult to control than one less so because of the difficulty of constructing effective preventive barriers against it.

All the factors discussed above must be considered in combination. I would suspect that other things being equal, a disease which was chronic, relatively severe, common, endemic, relatively contagious, with a simple host-to-host transmission pattern, discrete symptoms, and no animal reservoir would be the easiest to analyze, prevent, and eventually treat, given the availability of therapeutic materials. Alternatively, a mild, acute condition might not engender enough anxiety to be bothered with at all. A severe, epidemic, but relatively rare, sporadic, contagious, and acute disease, with a complex etiology and an animal reservoir population, should create difficulties for even the most sophisticated of medical systems.

Any analysis of disease adaptation would have to consider the range of permutations and combinations of these factors acting together. In addition, those factors which represent a continuum would have to be rated on a scale with different values for each disease. Such values would then have to be worked into a matrix of adaptation.

In most cases, particularly in non-Western populations, the factors outlined above should be expected to play a more important role in the development of preventive medicine than in the development of therapeutic devices. This is because these factors involve problems related to discovering the etiological agent of a disease and its maximal and minimal environmental requirements. The discovery of effective therapeutic methods depends upon further tests of the environment, involving potential medical preparations.

In addition to the characteristics outlined above, each of which is related to diseases as specific entities, complicating factors exist which make the problem of adaptation to disease even more difficult to unravel.

1. The general disease theory of a population may

turn it toward or away from the empirical investigation of pathologies. While some of the treatment or preventive measures developed for specific conditions might be isomorphic with effective Western medical practice, the reliance on too simple a theory or the inclusion of more material than is applicable to it may hinder the development of adequate discovery procedures. This problem has come up again and again in Western medicine. The early successes of the germ theory, for example, led to a great deal of noisy speculation in regard to conditions which were either genetic or nutritional in origin. As late as the nineteen twenties, medical researchers were still searching for the organism responsible for pellagra, a disease which turned out to be a vitamin deficiency. More recently genetic theories obscured the existence of slow viruses.

2. While preventive measures can be devised for all diseases, curative materials may just not exist in the environment. When they do exist, their discovery may prove highly difficult. Thus Eskimo populations have a much smaller choice of plant material to choose from in the development of a native pharmacopoeia than natives living in a tropical environment. In our own medical system at the present time, only a few effective therapeutic agents against viral diseases have been discovered.

3. Although there are exceptions discussed below, in general the longer a population has been in contact with a disease the less severe it becomes. This results from a dual process of accommodation between the organism and the host. A parasite which

does not kill its host is more likely to survive than one which literally eats itself out of house and home. Genetic change in the immunological patterns of all animal populations, including humans, is rather rapid when disease is the selective agent.

4. As I have already suggested, certain behaviors may increase the incidence of a particular pathology and yet remain fixed in a population. This may occur when such behaviors provide more gain than loss in the overall functioning of the socioeconomic system. The development of such minimax processes, in which gain and loss are balanced against each other, must itself take time, and therefore it should be possible to work such a concept into the adaptive model. When disease-promoting behaviors are present, other countermeasures may be developed to handle the inherent danger. Some groups which use fecal material as fertilizer, for example, store it for several days before use. Storage stimulates combustion in the manure and reduces the parasite population. The development of such compensatory behavior, however, makes the adaptation to disease a more complicated problem for the populations involved since it involves additional steps in the discovery process.

5. In many if not most cases of disease, the patient gets well regardless of, and sometimes in spite of, the particular therapy involved. Such spontaneous remissions add considerable noise to the system and can only serve to delay the development of effective therapeutic procedures. The only way around such a problem, which is further compounded by the so-called placebo effect, is to run a controlled experi-

ment with matched samples. This procedure is generally limited to Western medicine with its empirical orientation.

The analysis of adaptation to disease is both an evolutionary and an ethnohistorical problem. If the model of adaptation presented in this chapter is to prove useful, it must be tested cross culturally. That is, it must be shown to have some general validity. In general, cross cultural analysis can be made from existing ethnographic data, but in the case of adaptation to disease almost no such material exists. It is therefore necessary to build a sample of data on disease behavior from present and future field work. It is also necessary to gather more reliable information on the historical distributions of particular pathologies. This is a difficult but not impossible task. Several methods exist which in combination could produce some valid historical baselines for comparison.

PALEOPATHOLOGY

The first of these methods, paleopathology, is not new to anthropology. But work with archaic material has been limited. This is due in part to the relative lack of interest on the part of archaeologists and to a lack of professional skill in an area of physical anthropology which requires medical training. In addition, the types and number of diseases amenable to paleopathological analysis are limited. Recently a new interest in this field has developed (see Jarco 1966), and new techniques promise to increase the kind of disease data which may be extracted from archaeological material.

The major material for paleopathological analysis has been, and will always be, bone. Unfortunately, very few infectious diseases leave their marks on bone, and so only limited data can be extracted from it. Brothwell (1963), a leading English paleopathologist, lists the following diseases which can be analyzed from skeletal material:

1. *Inflammation of Bone.* Osteitis, periostitis, osteomyelitis, tuberculosis, syphilitic diseases of bone, leprosy, yaws.

2. *Tumors.* Osteomata (benign), sarcoma, carcinoma.

3. *Diseases of Joints.* Arthritis, osteo and rheumatoid.

4. *Diseases of Jaws and Teeth.* Caries, periodontal disease (tissue infection), abscesses, hypoplasia, cysts, odontomes (dental tumors).

5. *Deformities.* Polio, congenital dysplasia of the hip.

6. *Endocrine Changes.* Acromegaly, hypopituitarism.

7. *Effects of Diet on Bone.* Ricketts, osteomalacia (similar to rickets, lack of ability to calcify bone).

8. *Acquired Affections of Unknown Origin.* Paget's disease (occurs after fifty, affecting pelvis, tibia, lower spine and skull), osteoporosis (abnormally porous bone).

9. *Congenital Developmental Error.* Achondroplasia, hydrocephaly, acrocephaly, microcephaly.

10. *Synostoses of Unknown Origin.* Scaphocephaly

(long and narrow skull), trigonocephaly (narrow frontal bone), plagiocephaly (asymmetry of skull).

The only infectious diseases on this list are oste- itis, periostitis, osteomyelitis, tuberculosis, syphilis, leprosy, yaws, and poliomyelitis. Only the last five are caused by specific organisms, and even these often leave ambiguous markings. A known connec- tion between a genetic disorder and an infectious disease can be used in paleopathological analysis if the genetic disorder produces bone change. Recently Angel (1966) analyzed a series of skeletons from the Mediterranean area for bone changes caused by cer- tain genetically based hemoglobin variation patholo- gies associated with resistance to malaria. Changing distributions of such pathologies give strong evidence for an historical analysis of malarial distribution.

The contribution of paleopathology to the historical study of epidemic diseases can be enhanced through the study of other tissues, when they occur, and from the analysis of buried fecal material, politely referred to as coprolites by archaeologists. Dermal material often reveals bacterial infection, and coprolites can be successfully analyzed for a rather large series of helminthic infections.

CHARACTERISTICS OF DISEASE ORGANISMS THEMSELVES

Burnett (1966) has suggested, and others have agreed, that severe pathologies are recent in origin. He argued that selective pressures on parasites will tend to lower their pathogeneity to the point where they come into accommodation with their hosts. It has also been suggested that hosts develop resistance to their parasites. The historical rule of thumb provided by such a phenomenon would suggest that all relatively mild diseases are old for human populations, and severe diseases are recent in origin. From the point of view of the organism, reduced pathology is most beneficial when transfer from host to host is most difficult. In such cases the parasite population runs the risk of extinction each time host mortality is the outcome of a disease episode. On the other hand, parasites which are viable outside the host for long periods can remain relatively virulent and still operate successfully.

Several methods of survival appear to have evolved. Some viruses can remain viable indefinitely in a desiccated state, and many parasite species have remained virulent through time, although historical evidence attests to their antiquity. Certain bacteria and even protozoa are capable of entering a dormant state outside the host for varying periods. The tetanus bacillus sporalates itself and does not become active until it is injected deep into a puncture wound. Again, without modern therapy tetanus is a severe disease with very high mortality. Tuberculosis parasites are capable of sustaining themselves for several weeks to several months outside their hosts, depending on environmental conditions. Varying degrees of virulence displayed by this disease are probably due more to host factors than to genetic accommodation on the part of the parasite.

There are cases in which the biological characteristics of specific organisms can help the historical epidemiologist to determine whether or not a disease is recent in a particular geographic area.

In the case of the salmonella group responsible for typhoid, paratyphoid, and other salmonella-induced enteric diseases, the parasites pass through a sexual phase and are therefore highly mutable. A large number of strains have been typed. This fact is important to historical epidemiology because the techniques employed by botanists to identify the origin of plant species may be applied to these organisms. Botanical theory holds that the geographical origin of a species may be determined by finding the locus of the highest number of related wild subspecies (see Vavalov 1951). Where few species occur, it may be assumed that the plant is a recent introduction. As far as the salmonella organism is concerned, 636 phage types of the paratyphoid organism have been noted in India, while only three have been isolated in West Africa (May 1958:174). In this case the high number of phage types in India suggests Indian origin for the disease; the low number suggests recent introduction to West Africa.

The biology of plague also allows for some historical analysis. The disease has a short incubation period (two to six days), is very deadly, and is caused by an organism of low viability. Plague is likely to travel with rats rather than with men, and places where rats cannot go or could not go in the historical past would tend to be uninvolved in plague epidemics.

West Africa is such an area. Travelers carrying infected fleas across the Sahara would be unlikely to complete the journey. The carrier rat is not a desert dweller, and so it is unlikely that the plague could have reached the coast of West Africa before contact times when rats from infected ships could have swarmed ashore. There is one small endemic center for the plague in West Africa, located around Dakar, and another in central Africa. The spotty distribution of the disease suggests that the two centers are independent of each other. This supposition could be checked through analysis of the strains present in Africa. According to Burrows (1954:444-45):

A number of authors . . . have distinguished three physiological varieties of the plague bacillus. Variety I, *P.p. orientalis*, does not ferment glycerol but reduces nitrate; variety II, *P.p. antiqua*, ferments glycerol and reduces nitrate; and variety III, *P.p. mediaevalis*, ferments glycerol and does not reduce nitrate. The primary foci of infection of variety I are India, Burma and South China, and it is the agent of oriental plague, causing the 1894 epidemic and is also responsible for sylvatic or wild rodent plague in the U. S. Variety II, probably the oldest, came from Transbaikalia, Mongolia and Manchuria in central Asia, moved west with the Aryan invasions and followed the valley of the Nile into central Africa, leaving foci persisting to the present time. It also moved back toward the Mediterranean in the sixth century and is believed to be responsible for the Justinian plague that spread through the Roman Empire. It has since disappeared from Europe and has remained isolated in Africa. Variety III, possibly arising by a slow transformation of II, spread from the Caspian Sea throughout Europe causing the black death, and establishing itself in endemic foci.

Because of the nature of the organism and the problems involved in its transmission, I would suggest as a hypothesis that the strain of *Pasteurella pestis* endemic in the area around Dakar is the third (*P. p. mediaevalis*). If the hypothesis were correct, one would also expect plague to be a recent introduction to West Africa. (Reliable historical evidence so far places it only in northeast and central Africa.)

Other biological techniques no doubt exist which can be used to investigate the historical distribution of specific illnesses. These techniques will have to be applied pragmatically to each particular problem under investigation.

IMMUNOCHEMISTRY

The distribution of hereditary resistance should be of value in deciphering the disease history of a population. Several attempts at this type of analysis have been made. Unambiguous results are difficult to obtain, however, since disease can act as a rapid agent of selection, particularly when it produces high mortality among individuals before they reach reproductive age. Date-specific hypotheses are therefore difficult to prove with this method. On the other hand, if applied with caution, it has great value for the investigation of geographic distributions of pathologies.

Certain tantalizing possibilities for historical epidemiology exist within the area of blood group genetics and hemoglobin systems. There appear to be chemical similarities between the structures of antigens carried on red blood cells and certain species of bacteria, for example. Some authors have suggested that susceptibility to plague bacteria and smallpox is closely related to the distribution of blood groups which do not carry the H specific antigen and are similar to the antigenic properties of *Pasteurella pestis* as well as the smallpox virus. This point of view is clearly summarized by Otten (1967) in an article critical of such work.

According to the hypotheses of these several writers, individuals are immunologically handicapped in antibody production against virus or bacteria which carry antigenic specificities similar to those of their own blood group substances. In other words, the closer the structural correspondence between ABH and microbial capsular antigens, the poorer the resources for resistance in the host. Further by virtue of his "normal" blood group anti-A and/or anti-B antibodies, an individual may be equipped with built-in protection against a certain category of organisms. Blood group antigenic specificities, it should be recalled, are not limited to the erythrocyte membrane, but are apparently attributes of glycolipoid complexes characterizing a great variety of cells and tissues . . . H. A. and/or B antigens also appear in soluble mucopolysaccharide form in most secretions of those individuals (by far the majority of the world's inhabitants) who carry the secretor (Se) gene in either homozygous or heterozygous combination. Blood group specificity may accordingly be thought of as characterizing the entire organism rather than only certain components of the blood stream. (Otten 1967:210)

The author goes on to criticize present studies in this area because in her terms the data do not match the expected blood group frequencies.

Plague ravaged areas, which should, according to Vogel, demonstrate high A and/or B frequencies at the expense of O, can be reconstructed for much of eastern Asia and Turkey. Africa, however, does not comply, being a mixed bag of ABO frequencies, the incidence of the A gene being generally lower than in Europe and the O gene often in considerable prominence, especially in the populous old Guinea Coast Kingdoms. (Otten 1967:210)

It may be that my own hypothesis, that plague is not in fact native to West Africa, might have something to do with ABO frequencies in that area, but Otten is certainly correct when she cites data relating to the frequency of smallpox and the O gene in the New World.

Other authors have attempted to explain the distributions of the ABO(H) system on the basis of polymorphisms involving chronic disorders of one type or another (see Buettner-Janusch 1958). This evidence is difficult to accept because of the disorders listed most affect individuals rather late in life and therefore would not be expected to lower fertility. Still, even a small change in selective values can produce shifts in gene frequency, and these hypotheses cannot be ruled out. Otten, in the paper cited above, suggests still another area in which antigenic agents of the host might be related to resistance to specific diseases.

Here we consider another area of immunological activity, the lower reaches of the gastrointestinal tract. The contents include a potpourri of gamma globulins . . . enormous bacterial populations, living and dead, representing a number of types and species; several enzymes and other agents poured into the tract via exocrine ducts

104

and secreting surfaces; mucous secretions carry soluble A, B, H, and Lewis blood group polysaccharides in impressive amounts; and the residues of diet itself. (Otten 1967:214)

No one has yet ventured to suggest an association between blood group frequency and diet by way of the gut but several factors indicate a look in this direction may not be completely unwarranted. *Escherichia coli* and the Proteus ("Putrifying") group, both largely associated with a carnivorous diet, are reported to carry B antigenic activity, at least in some strains. . . . Do then blood type B individuals make better carnivores than blood type A folk? Do intestinal environments differ immunologically with regard to their receptivity to one organism or another? Will one species of microbe, more easily established for immunological reasons increase the growth and vitality of its particular host, while another species proves deleterious? These questions strain our knowledge too far, but I believe they may well be kept in mind in approaching the larger problem of natural selection in man. (Otten 1967:215)

Better evidence exists for a genetic relationship between certain blood pathologies such as sickle cell anemia, thalassemia and G6PD deficiency, and resistance to disease. All these conditions arise from a genetically based alteration of the hemoglobin molecule. All are implicated in resistance to malaria. In the case of sickle cell anemia the evidence for resistance to infectious disease is rather elegant, but we must not lose sight of the fact that this is the only good example available at the present time. I have yielded, as have many authors, to the temptation to pull these genetic diseases out of the hat like so many rabbits to prove a point for which there is little evidence in any other area of pathology.

Still another line of attack on possible relationships between blood groups, antibodies, and infectious disease has been taken by Gorman (1964). He suggests a relationship between malaria and selection against the Rh-negative factor. Gorman reasons that the better antibody formers within a population are those most likely to survive malarial attack. Thus malaria would select for good antibody formers. At the same time good antibody formers are more likely to produce erythroblastosis in the case of Rh incompatibility. The side effect of this double selection would then be the reduction of Rh-negative individuals in the population.

Gorman admits that malaria is not the only disease implicated in such a hypothesis but considers it to be of major importance in tropical environments because it affects a large number of individuals and tends to kill children before reproductive age. An examination of the frequency of the Rh-negative gene yields the following distribution:

> In general it is a common gene in northern peoples, less common in Mediterranean, African, Middle Eastern and Indian peoples, rare in oriental peoples and absent from Melanesians and the Australian Aborigines. . . . It can be seen from these figures that if only populations which have a large pool of Rh-negative genes are considered there is a remarkable geographical correlation between: (1) the degree of depression of the Rh-negative gene frequency from the European level of 0.38; (2) the geographical incidence of one or other of the genes like the haemoglobin S gene which are already considered to be selected for by malaria; (3) the world distribution of malaria. The

106

correlation of (2) and (3) is already well known, and it is clear from the foregoing observations that (1) correlates equally well.

It is likely that in those peoples with a zero Rh-negative gene frequency the absence of the Rh-negative gene is due to the fact that it was never present in the first place, rather than it has been selected out completely by erythro-blastosis foetalis. Such populations are therefore irrelevant to the theory. (Gorman 1964:678)

Elizabeth Szinyei-Merse has suggested that the so-called "founder effect" might be used to unravel the disease history of parent populations. She reasoned that a high frequency of genetic resistance to disease in a small island population no longer exposed to the specific pathology might provide some evidence of past experience with the condition. The demonstration of such a genetic mechanism in only one island population might be attributed to chance, but its occurrence in several such groups, all of which are known to have sprung from the same parental population, would be highly suggestive. The hypothesis becomes particularly interesting if the founder gene is no longer found in the parental population. Such a result would suggest a shift in selective pressures, that is, a change in the disease history of a population.

It should be painfully obvious that all the hypotheses discussed here are highly speculative. Simple correlations between particular conditions and the frequency of some genetically controlled system will be difficult to assess until some biochemical links can be demonstrated as an explanation. Nonetheless this area of research looks highly promising for future studies of historical epidemiology, particularly when such distributions correlate with other types of evidence.

HISTORICAL RECORDS

Written documents should be the best source of information on disease history. But in many cases they do not cover those populations crucial to the kind of investigation suggested in this chapter. In addition many early descriptions of disease are either vague or misleading. Only a few of the early explorers were trained in diagnosis of disease, and even these were often content with such statements as "the natives suffer from certain fluxes and fevers." No matter how quaint, this type of description is useless for historical analysis. On the other hand, new diseases might be documented, particularly if the symptoms were strange to the observer and/or at the same time strikingly clear and easy to describe. Mungo Park (1801) mentions guinea worm (dracuntiasis), yaws, and elephantiasis in his *Travels and Recent Discoveries in the Interior Districts of Africa in the Years 1796 and 1797*. Such documentation is probably quite accurate.

Fairly good descriptions exist for such diseases as smallpox, tuberculosis, rabies, hepatitis (at least in India), and various parasites. The word leprosy, however, has changed its meaning since its first biblical descriptions.

HOST SPECIFICITY
AND PARASITE STRAINS

In general, diseases specific to human hosts are considered to be younger than those which affect a wide range of infrahuman species. This does not give much indication of the antiquity of the disease in human populations, however. In some cases it is possible to relate the distribution of related parasite types, their hosts, the geographic origin of a particular pathology, and the relative date of its spread to a new geographical area.

In an interesting paper, "On the Antiquity of Malaria in the Western Hemisphere," Dunn (1965) offers an analysis of this type which may be taken as a model for research into other parasitic diseases.

First of all Dunn links the absence of malaria-related polymorphisms in the New World to recent introduction (this has already been discussed above), but he demands further evidence: "Were there, or were there not, malaria parasites infective for man in the Americas prior to European contact?" Dunn goes on to point out that in Africa and Asia, malaria parasites of the genus *Plasmodium* have been recorded for man and many species of infrahuman primates and other old world mammals. In the Americas, parasites have been recorded only for man and the cebid monkeys. In addition, Dunn mentions another parasite, genus *Hepatocystis*, which occurs in Old World mammals, including monkeys, but not in man or the anthropoid apes. The four species of *Plas-*

modium known occur in both the Old and the New World, while the cebid parasites have been named *P. brasilianum* and *P. simium*. *P. brasilianum* is very similar morphologically to *P. malariae*, one of the human types, while *P. simium* appears to be closely related to *P. vivax*, also a human type. In addition, no parasite resembling *P. falciparum* was found in "free ranging Neo-tropical primates and laboratory attempts to transmit such an organism to cebids are unsuccessful."

Dunn concludes with this hypothesis:

Neither man nor monkey harbored malaria parasites in the New World in pre-Columbian times. *P. malariae* and *P. vivax* evolved in Old World higher primates and were brought by man to the Western Hemisphere, where new anopheline vectors transmitted the plasmodia to aboriginal and colonial man and to some of the more receptive platyrrhines (i.e., a "reverse" zoonosis). Any minor changes that have occurred in morphology and physiology have been the product of four and a half centuries of adaptation to the cebid host. The *P. malariae* strains, inadvertantly introduced into cebid populations, are today described as *P. brasilianum*, while the *P. vivax* strains are known today as *P. simium*. (Possibly the names *P. brasilianum* and *P. simium* will eventually be suppressed as synonyms when more extensive morphological, physiological and cross transmission experiments have been conducted. (Dunn 1965:388)

The technique of analysis applied by Dunn should be applicable to a fairly wide range of protozonal and helminthic parasites as well as some bacterial species. Such research could go a long way in expanding our knowledge of early disease distributions.

VECTOR DISTRIBUTIONS

Livingstone's classic paper (1958) links culturally induced changes in the available vector environment to the spread of falciparum malaria in West Africa. This kind of analysis can undoubtedly be expanded to other diseases. One case might be schistosomiasis. The introduction of wet rice agriculture into an area is often related to the expansion of schistosoma-bearing snails. Such vectors are highly sensitive to breeding conditions. They favor mildly flowing water and do poorly in both swift streams and stagnant pools. Mozley (1963) points out that irrigation ditches and other man-made water courses provide a perfect environment for the reproduction of such organisms. The disease continues to spread today in such constructions as road culverts and dammed areas.

Most vectors have rather specific ecological requirements which can be improved or destroyed by man-induced alterations of the environment. Careful study of these requirements in combination with archaeological research has rarely been attempted, although it offers obvious advantages for historical epidemiology.

LINGUISTIC EVIDENCE

The collection of disease vocabularies in particular language family areas might be used as an index of relative age for specific conditions. Disease terms which are widely distributed and are not cognate with the language of recent colonizers would provide some indication of antiquity. Borrowed disease terms might indicate recent introduction. Problems exist with this technique, to be sure. Rapid medical acculturation might lead to replacement of vocabulary terms in the native language with Western terms. This factor can be considered, however, in the course of ethnographic analysis. If a linguistic area is large, the zone of cognates might also prove interesting, showing a geographic distribution limited to part of an area. The existence of native terminology in one zone and borrowed terminology in another might indicate that a particular disease has spread only since the period of colonization.

At the present time very few linguists have collected and published disease terminologies. Most vocabulary lists include only a few scattered disease terms and many of these are general, such as the word for fever or sore or headache. In addition, since few linguists, or ethnologists for that matter, can be expected to provide accurate diagnosis of disease, the translations of disease might prove to be inaccurate. It is therefore necessary that such linguistic evidence be collected with the cooperation of medical specialists. This is not as difficult as it may sound. The work can be done in a local hospital with the anthropologist comparing native terms to Western diagnosis on the spot.

None of the techniques discussed in this chapter are simple, nor is it possible that a single anthropologist could be well versed in all of them. The investigation of a particular historical problem, however, can be pursued with the aid of existing archival data, plus a good deal of sleuthing on the part of the investigator. When these techniques are combined, the number of diseases which can be investigated becomes rather impressive. In such cases when various techniques yield the same result for a particular condition the quest for historical accuracy is furthered.

CHAPTER 5

NATIVE MEDICAL
PRACTICE

DIAGNOSTICS

In general, diseases which are ethnically defined as common, and mild conditions of short duration are either self-diagnosed or, if a child's disease, diagnosed and treated by the parents or some near relative. Mild conditions which persist may provoke anxiety but, if they are also common, may be classified outside the realm of disease and either ignored or self-treated in a rather haphazard manner. The severity of the symptoms which will be endured, however, depends on such cultural factors as definitions of illness and such physiological factors as pain threshold, as well as upon ecological conditions such as overall disease incidence, frequency of illness in the community, and the types of disease prevalent. In much of West Africa, for example, yaws is endured, but in the United States it would undoubtedly arouse great anxiety and lead to professional treatment. This is a combined ethnosemantic and ecological problem. Research on individual medical system as well as cross cultural studies are needed to unravel it. I would think that certain environmental parameters would in fact influence culturally defined choices.

When a disease is defined as serious, an affected individual or his family may seek help from an outside specialist. The first type of person consulted is generally in the class of nonprofessional expert who because of age and/or experience has a greater than average knowledge of curing practices. Frequently such individuals are secular curers, and they rarely do more than diagnose the condition on the basis of symptoms and prescribe some simple medication. Among the Abron of West Africa there are many such individuals. Most of them are older members of the community, and many are women who have raised a high percentage of their offspring to maturity. My classificatory mother was widely respected in the community because she had not "lost" any of her nine children. She was consulted frequently, particularly about childhood illness.

If a disease is severe, chronic, or exotic, an affected individual will probably seek out professional advice. As in Western society, the first problem is one of diagnosis. Diagnostic techniques vary from culture to culture and from specialist to specialist where different types are found within the same cultural tradition.

The diagnostic process is frequently complicated. In some medical systems attention may be paid to the particular symptoms, but the practitioner will frequently need more information than an examination of the sick individual can provide. This is because the diagnostician is usually charged with discovering the social cause of the disease. Symptoms are one clue and sometimes are in fact taken as a sign of some particular condition, but more often the medical specialist must consult the supernatural. A sick individual is somehow out of balance with supernatural forces. His disease may be due to the attack of living or dead enemies, malevolent ghosts, supernatural beings such as gods, devils, goblins, or witches, or because of some breach of taboo. In the case of attack, the medical specialist must act in some way to counteract the evil force. In the case of breach of taboo or some insult of supernatural powers, the practitioner must counsel his patient as to what kind of supplication will be necessary for the restoration of health.

A widespread diagnostic process consists of consultation with the supernatural through the offices of a medium or directly through a trance state. Such diagnosis procedures are found throughout the non-Western world. Another familiar technique consists of divination through some random process such as scapolamancy, throwing the bones, or the examination of some natural object such as the liver of a chicken. Such a system may have important non-medical functions (see Chapter 6), but it tends to reduce the effectiveness of specific diagnosis. Only patient-centered medical examinations allow medical practice to develop some kind of empirically based category system, which in turn can lead to experimentation with drugs used consistently for a specific set of symptoms. The relating of causality to the supernatural can hinder such a process because it tends to remove symptoms from the main line of information. Nonetheless, where symptoms are clear-cut and diseases fairly common, many societies have developed a consistent set of treatments specific to the symptoms themselves.

Whether or not these medications are effective is another question; efficacy depends upon the limitations placed on the medical system by the availability of certain natural and artificial products in the environment within the framework of the technological system. In some societies symptoms call for the prescription of specific palliatives while divination gets at the "root" of the illness. Thus the disease is treated socially and medically. When patients display multiple symptoms, for example headache, fever, or rash, these are frequently treated as separate entities. Such single symptom-oriented therapy tends to work against the development of a sophisticated diagnostic system in which the permutation and combination of symptoms are considered. It would therefore be interesting to compare the efficacity of those medical systems which treat whole syndromes with those which treat each symptom separately. It is my impression, however, that the vast majority of non-peasant indigenous medical systems ignore syndromes as entities. This is a point which can be judged only through further research.

MEDICATION

While some medicines have a demonstrably direct and positive physiological effect, frequently no empirical connection exists between a specific disease and the chemical constituents of a particular medication. In such cases the only possible effect is psychosomatic. Most if not all native medicines are unmodified plant, animal, or mineral products. Such materials may undergo an extractive process such as grinding or boiling, while others may be dissolved in water or in alcohol, but it is unlikely that new chemical combinations are produced even in the frequent mixing processes which occur. The development of complicated drugs requires a technological system and a scientific point of view. These are generally lacking in the medical systems of non-Western societies. However, there are several natural products which are effective against particular symptoms such as aches, diarrhea, and swelling, and a few which ameliorate specific diseases. Following Githens (1948), these may be classified according to their chemical constituents:

Fats and Oils. These may be used externally or internally. External use is generally restricted to local irritations or for cosmetic effects. Internally certain oils, particularly castor oil, may be used as cathartics; others are antihelminthic in their action.

Glucosides. Complex chemical structures which can be subclassified into a number of medicinal types:

1. *Tannins.* These products, common in bark and tea, are capable of constricting blood vessels and of precipitating proteins and mucous. They may therefore be used in cases of hemorrhage and bleeding ulcers. Tannins are also effective against burns since

they tend to restrict the ooze of plasma from the damaged tissue. They may also be effective against diarrhea.

2. *Saponins*. These have a detergent action and may, like soap, be used as emetics. They also tend to stimulate mucous secretion and may serve as effective expectorants. The nausea which accompanies the action of emetics tends to cause sweating, which in turn has an effect on febrile conditions.

3. *Antihelminthic glucosides*. These form a small group of glucosides which tend to kill and expel intestinal parasites.

4. *Salicylic glucosides*. All related to aspirin, and common in willow leaves, these medicinal plants have been known for a long time in Europe and Africa. They provide one of the most widespread types of medication.

5. *Neurotoxic glucosides*. These are narcotic and are employed as mild relaxants for the intestinal tract.

Mucilages and Gums. These are related to starches. All are bland and soothing for such conditions as stomach ache and heartburn, particularly in pregnant women.

Alkaloids. These are dangerous drugs. Among them is the hallucinogen peyote which is actually a conglomeration of several alkaloids. Some alkaloids may be used to stimulate urine flow and reduce liquid content in the body, others are used against fevers.

Essential Oils. These include volatile, strongly scented liquids like banana oil. Some may check bacterial growth and can be used as wound dressings.

Resins. Irritating substances which may be used as counterirritants and as emetics.

Sulphur Oils. Highly irritating oils like mustard oil, which may be used as counterirritants and as emetics.

Anthraquinone Cathartics. A group of mild purges which may also be used as dressings for wounds and burns.

For obvious reasons peoples living in a tropical climate are more likely to develop a large *materia medica* than those restricted to areas with impoverished flora. The Abron of the Ivory Coast have at least one hundred and fifty-one plant medications to which must be added several types of clay and minerals. Of these, thirteen are used to cure dysentery and diarrhea, ten are used for leprosy, ten for edema, nine as analgesics, eight for sores, eight for cough and bronchial conditions, and eight as purgatives. In all, thirty-eight different pathological states are treated with drug plants, but most of them are conditions or symptoms rather than specific diseases (spasms, sores, pain, edema, cough, fever, eye irritations). In cases of specific diseases, medicines are earmarked for conditions which in fact have very clear symptomologies, including leprosy, venereal disease, yaws, scabies, tropical ulcers, elephantiasis, sleeping sickness, snakebite, and sterility. Yellow fever is also on the list, but it is the only disease singled out from a large group of fevers which are prevalent in the area.

Other medicines are used to produce clinical effects in patients, acting as purgatives or aiding in birth, combating fatigue, giving strength, stimulating the production of milk, or acting as aphrodisiacs. Mineral products such as clay are used in the treatment of smallpox and chickenpox.

In Ponape, Riesenberg (1948) lists seventy-one types of medication for twenty-seven conditions. Such medical problems as sterility, contraception, and childbirth are also dealt with. The largest number of treatments, four, are for gonorrhea and for wounds caused by poisonous fish. Three types of treatment are used for tetanus, abnormal menstruation, female uterine problems, headache, fever, vomiting, diarrhea, bruises, abscesses, and a disease known as disease of mangroves. Again, most of these conditions relate to specific symptoms rather than to diseases and to external irritations rather than to serious internal conditions.

William Mitchell, who has done excellent field work among the Aymara Indians of Bolivia, collected fifty-five plants used for medicinal purposes. Of these, several were used for wounds and boils, and each of the following conditions had five methods of treatment: fevers, stomach pains, uterine contractions, pain, fractures, and swellings. Other conditions treated included constipation, "liver upsets," irritations, rheumatism, obesity, helminths, colds and bronchial infections, and heart conditions. Mitchell found that more than one half of the plants used are traditional in Spanish medicine and may have their roots in the European homeopathic tradition.

Aymara medicine fits the patterns described for Abron and Ponape. Diseases with highly discrete symptomologies or nonspecific conditions are diagnosed and treated with available medicinal material. The use of medication is restricted by the limitations of naturally occurring drugs, and the diagnostic procedures are often hampered by the methods employed in treatment.

While the Abron use medication externally as well as internally, some peoples tend to restrict medicinal use to external application. Georgeda Bick (personal communication) has informed me that the Maring of Eastern New Guinea rarely take medicine internally. Whiting and Child (1953), in an extensive study of child training and personality, have suggested that customs relating to illness can be used as indices of culturally determined personality characteristics. For a sample of seventy-five societies, Whiting and Child found that only forty took medicines internally by swallowing. The authors reasoned that therapeutic practices would be "directly influenced by explanations of illness." (Whiting and Child 1953:206)

We picked out six other instances where it seemed likely that the presence of a particular explanation of illness would lead to the adoption of a corresponding item of therapeutic practice. These instances are as follows:

1. A belief that illness is produced by ingestion of something might lead to vomiting as a means of getting rid of the noxious substances.

2. The same belief also seems likely to lead to the therapeutic observances of food taboos as a means of preventing worsening or recurrence of the illness through repeated ingestion of the dangerous material.

3. Attribution of illness to sexual behavior should favor sexual abstinence as a therapeutic practice.

4. Similarly, attribution of illness to sexual behavior

should favor observance of specific sexual taboos as a therapeutic practice.

5. Where illness is blamed on the patient's having lost something or having had something removed from his body, therapy might be expected to be directed at restoring or replacing whatever has been lost or removed.

6. Where illness is believed to be brought about by the magical introduction of some object or spirit into the patient's body, therapy might be expected to involve an effort to remove this alien object or spirit.

In each of these six cases we have tested whether societies which have the specified explanation of illness are thereby more likely to have the therapeutic practice which seemed to correspond. In every one of the six cases we found a positive relationship. It is surprising that only one of the six relationships is large enough to be statistically significant. With respect to the general point that therapeutic practices are influenced by explanations of illness, however, the uniform direction of these six associations and the five previously reported is an impressive finding (though the fact that several of the associations involve the same measures prevents a statistical evaluation of this over-all finding). (Whiting and Child 1953: 207-08)

The authors were particularly concerned with what they refer to as positive and negative fixation in personality development. According to their theory, positive fixation results from overindulgence at a particular stage of development and produces projective systems in which phenomena are explained and problems solved in terms of the particular level of fixation. Negative fixation is hypothesized as the result of unpleasant experiences during a particular level of socialization. It is suggested that positive fixation finds its outlet in medical systems in terms of par-

123

ticular forms of "performance therapies." Such therapies provide a source of security. Negative fixation produces what the authors refer to as "avoidance therapies." These therapies were classified as follows:

Oral avoidance therapies—spitting, vomiting and adherence to food taboos.

Anal avoidance therapies—retention of feces, washing or cleansing and adherence to cleanliness taboos.

Sexual avoidance therapies—general sexual abstention, or adherence to specific sexual taboos.

Dependence avoidance therapies—therapeutic practices which involve isolating the patient or removing him from his home for the duration of his illness.

Aggression avoidance therapies—the sacrifice of property as a therapeutic device, or therapeutic practices which take the form of attempts to placate agent responsible for the illness. (Whiting and Child 1953:209-10)

Particular psychological orientations of the type suggested by these authors may affect the sort of treatment favored by a people and restrict the range of natural products within the environment which will be used as medication. On the other hand, discovery procedures may exist within the behavioral system which increase the possibility that empirically valid medicines will be found. On Ponape, for example (Riesenberg 1948), much attention is paid to the behavior of sick dogs. If such an animal is seen to eat a particular plant and then recovers, the plant is tried by humans. This is certainly a good example of "natural science" in action. On the other hand, natives of Ponape also search out new forms of therapy through dreams. According to Riesenfeld, individuals often attempt to direct their dreaming towards the discovery of new medicines. If, as is likely, the dream content of a people is highly patterned, such behavior may orient therapeutic discoveries in a particular direction. Since idiosyncratic elements probably turn up in individual dreams, however, such a procedure can be expected to randomize medicinal choices to some extent and, therefore, widen the experimental field.

The Abron of the Ivory Coast live in close proximity to many other cultural traditions and display a willing eclectiveness in their religious and medical behavior. New medicines are accepted from the outside at a startling rate. While the average Abron tires of a therapeutic technique which does not produce rather immediate effects, the Abron pharmacopoeia is open and in a state of constant change.

Such an openness towards new medicines is not a constant feature of all populations. Some are quite rigid in regard to change, and it is likely that in such groups new medicines become part of medical knowledge at a slow rate. Among the Ingalic (Northern Athabaskan Indians, Osgood 1959) treatment of major illnesses consists of shamanistic performances, or the use of curing songs which are sold as commodities. These tend to be scarce items of considerable value. The situation is complicated by the existence of good and bad songs. An individual with a bad song may attempt to foist it upon an unsuspecting person, often offering it for a low price. Both the scarcity of songs, and the possibility that a bargain can be worse than no song at all, must contribute to the price structure of such items. It is also likely that such a system tends to be conservative: keeping the supply of good songs low and therefore maintaining their price structure. The existence of such a procedure might also tend to turn therapeutic practices away from commonly available plant and mineral materials. In fact, several authors have noted that Northern Athabaskans make little use of plants in the treatment of disease. In Ponape, where empiricism is an active part of medical practice, medicines are also important commodities. But on Ponape it is plants themselves which make up the *materia medica*. While a supply of songs is potentially infinite, the supply of plants, particularly in an island environment, is limited. Early European folk medicine is peculiarly democratic in that almost all, if not all, common plants, including garden weeds and grasses, are used in therapy for one disease or another. I would suggest that the source of treatment (natural vs. artificial), the place of therapy in the economic structure, the overall availability of potential medicines, and the general attitude toward change within the behavioral system all contribute to the type and degree of medical innovation present.

In some societies exotic plants, or those which have some property valued in medical practice, such as irritants, aromatics, or amenability to sympathetic magic (red for blood, green to counter thick blood, as in Galanic medicine), are the prime choice. In other societies practically every plant or mineral material, including urine and feces, may be included.

Some of the problems involved in the development of effective medical practice have already been outlined in Chapter 4. I am convinced that the major difficulties in therapeutic techniques center around the general lack of a scientific methodology in preliterate societies. This is not to say that "primitive" man is nonempirical or prelogical. Such an attitude towards the thought and behavior of non-Western peoples has been demolished by a long and distinguished line of anthropologists. All human beings are imbedded in a natural setting, from which they gain information to be used in the development of techniques for coping with environmental difficulties, as well as for the extraction of energy.

The whole history of man writ large has been a process of adaptation in which culturally based behavior has been the major tool in the adjustment to, and the shaping of, the environment. Nonetheless, a specific feature of Western culture has been an externally oriented and empirically based technology and science. The major aspect of its success has been the development of a consistent set of methodological rules codified in the scientific method. Applied to disease and medicine, this orientation, particularly when combined with a highly involved technology, must inevitably lead to the development of a rational and effective medicine. Without such a methodology the cues available in the external world for the delineation of cause and the discovery of effective treatment are obscured by a high noise level. This noise level is due to difficulties of diagnosis where internal conditions produce only vague somatic symptoms, and where it is extremely difficult to distinguish one set of symptoms from another. The noise level is increased to crescendo by the fact that most patients get well regardless of therapy. The situation is further complicated by psychosomatic factors. These make it extremely difficult to discover which, if any, forms of treatment are effective. Of course the noise level can be reduced through carefully structured and controlled experiments, but this is precisely the point where non-Western medicine in most cases falls below the mark of the required objectivism and empirical orientation.

Non-Western medical specialists generally practice within a social context which makes nonmedical demands upon them. They are social adjudicators as well as religious functionaries whose duty it is to restore relationships between men, or between men and the supernatural. As such they treat social cause rather than disease. In addition the limited range of treatment products available to them, frequently coupled with diagnostic systems which tend to limit treatment to symptoms rather than to the underlying pathological condition, puts severe restraints upon the development of scientific medicine.

PREVENTIVE MEDICINE

Although much research needs to be done on this question it is my impression that preventive medicine as a system qua system is even more rudimentary in non-Western society than therapy. While quarantine in one form or another exists for some highly infectious diseases, and vaccination against smallpox (and in some societies snakebite) is known, most behavior constituting the "emic" framework of preventive medicine consists of various forms of charms and amulets which are believed to ward off evil spirits or other agents of disease. The observance of taboos the breach of which are believed to produce disease may be effective in preventing certain conditions, but these are often linked to conservation and social control rather than to the actual prevention of specific diseases. Such taboos might nonetheless be included in some ethnoscientific analysis of disease theory, and such behavior may in fact be adaptive in the medical sense.

If ethnoscience is ignored, however, and a grid defining preventive medicine in our own terms (see Chapter 8) is placed over the entire behavioral system of a population, several items of behavior will emerge which act to limit the occurrence of spread of specific diseases. Likewise, certain units of behavior which might at first glance appear to run counter to good health practice might well fit under the rubric of adaptation as defined in Chapter 2. I would expect that much (certainly not all) of what appears to be irrational behavior will turn out to fit the prevailing ecological conditions and demonstrate that much of behavior is either health oriented or produces maximization in some other way. An ethnoscientific analysis of medically oriented behavior will miss much of this material because it restricts itself to what the natives themselves define as medicine.

I am convinced from my own field research in West Africa and from the meager literature on hygiene and health in preliterate societies that the most effective behaviors in relation to disease actually fall under the rubric of preventive medicine as it has been defined here rather than under native medical theory of disease, treatment, or disease prevention. Information on cultural breakdown due to war or rapid culture change suggests that under such conditions disease rates and mortality go up. A general breakdown in the cultural system destroys a set of barriers to disease which developed through positive feedback. There is some evidence that even under conditions in which native medical systems remain unchanged disruptions in other areas of behavior have a profound effect on rates of pathology.

Without a scientific theory of medicine, feedbacks in the therapeutic system are obscured by the social aspect of therapy and by the frequent spontaneous recovery of individuals. The native therapist is limited by his own medical theory when he is faced with a sick person. The situational context of disease and the responses required are patterned by the semantic field which that context demands.

This is much less the case in preventive medicine. While the process of immunization is complicated by the same technological needs that are described for treatment, alternate methods of disease prevention abound. The context of such behavior is not restrained by disease theory or by specific encounters with disease. Items of behavior in the general stream of interaction with the environment may have a chance effect on disease rates. Those which are positive may then become fixed in the behavioral system. Positive feedback in such cases would operate outside disease theory but nonetheless have profound effects on rates of pathology within the population. In short, looking at native systems from the inside suggests that ethnomedical theories can have a restricting effect on the development of both therapy and preventive medicine. The latter, however, is freed somewhat from these restrictions, because much of the behavior objectively associated with health and disease lies outside the ethnomedical system.

All systems which direct behavior tend to limit responses. Behaviors become patterned according to this or that theory. If the theory is powerful, well and good. Feedback is actually speeded up, but if the theory is faulty, feedback may be slowed. In this situation, no theory, or a lack of connection between a specific theory and behavior, may be more effective in producing adaptive results. In addition, preventive medicine is inherently easier than treatment. There are fewer steps in the discovery process. Preventive medicine in the objective sense is thus a more open system.

In situations in which minimax choices have been made which increase productivity and/or carrying capacity of the environment but also increase disease rates, modifications of the maximization behavior may also occur, but those which decrease effectiveness of the maximization are likely to be rejected. Those which maintain the original adaptation but reduce disease at the same time are likely to become fixed in the behavioral system. Thus the use of human fecal material in high density areas increases disease risk, but the storage of such material for varying lengths of time (depending upon the disease) reduces such risk. Many cultures use raw human manure and therefore run a high risk. The Japanese, however, store such material and reduce its potentially dangerous effect. Such modifications of behavior will depend not only upon positive feedback but on such factors as overall population density, available land, and available storage areas. Some populations may not be able to afford the disease-reducing aspects of such modification.

No study has ever examined the overall health system of a population, much less the relationships of such a system to such problems as economic productivity. Nor have any researchers to my knowledge ever considered the possible stabilizing effects of disease on population numbers in areas where rising population size might contribute to the degradation of the environmental setting. Such population control must also be worked into the adaptive model, since successful adaptation may also include a significant degree of population loss under the techno-environmental conditions of a specific population. The loss of individuals to a population through disease may be much more acceptable than either infanticide or gerontocide. Data suggest that in most cultures in which infanticide is practiced, the killing of the newborn comes as a last resort and is highly disturbing to mothers. The killing of old people, in addition to the psychological problem which it may engender, can deprive the group of valuable information stored in the minds of those who have had long and wide experience (see Laughlin 1962). Disease and death upset all people to some degree, but disease at least provides some external source of population control; one which does not demand sanctioned homicide. In addition, therapeutic procedures, no matter how ineffective, serve to reinforce social solidarity. In many cases it is not the efficacy of treatment that counts but the fact that treatment takes place at all.

CHAPTER 6
NATIVE MEDICAL SYSTEMS

Ethnographic descriptions of medical practice are rare in the anthropological literature. The major monographs in this area all come from Africa (Field 1937, Harley 1941, Gelfand 1965). On the other hand, the literature is full of specialized accounts of one or another aspect of medicine such as witchcraft and sorcery, medicine and social control, and ritual practice. In addition many standard ethnographies contain descriptions of curing practice occasionally enhanced by a partial specification of the native pharmacopoeia. Regardless of the incomplete and scattered nature of the literature, the relative ineffectiveness of non-Western medical practice tends to emerge from these accounts. This in spite of the romantic notion that a vast pharmacopoeia of undiscovered cures exists among the preliterate peoples of the world. If this is true then what can be said about the important place medicine and medical practitioners occupy in almost all societies?

First of all, one must begin with the truism that disease and death are universally anxiety provoking, if in varying degrees. It is this anxiety which provides the raw material for the development of medical practice. Second, the simple facts that most pathological conditions are self-limiting and that spontaneous remission is a frequent outcome of illness tend to generate confidence in the practitioner even when the empirical basis of his medicine is quite meager.

The probability that a significant amount of disease is psychosomatic in origin and that symptom remission may occur as the result of psychological factors, particularly those associated with the act of therapy, creates a situation in which the style of practice may be of greater importance than the type of medication employed. Thus while the development of effective organic therapy is slowed by the noise in the system, the feedbacks to the practitioner indicating what are psychologically effective behaviors in the therapeutic situation are probably quite rapid. This is supported by the fact that while therapeutic techniques vary among populations, practically everywhere the "medicine men" surround their practice with a mystique obviously calculated to produce awe in the patient. The status of curer carries not only an appropriate affect, but a technology which includes incantations, mysterious objects, and behavioral techniques which change the doctor's social personality and remove him from the normal social context. I think it is of extreme importance, for example, that the phenomenon of trance is so widespread in the diagnosis and treatment of disease. The trance state automatically transcends ordinary experience and opens a communication link with the supernatural. It also often plays a role in the discovery of medicines.

The fact that so many aspects of medical practice in one social group would be familiar to individuals in another social group cannot be gratuitous. It must represent a widespread adaptive trend based on rather effective positive feedback. Such feedback is most likely to be successful in the area of psychosomatic medicine because extraneous factors are shut out of the system.

While Western medical categories may be used effectively in ecological analysis, their use in the description of native medical practice must be more circumscribed. Although prophylaxis and/or treatment of pathological conditions are the general semantic and pragmatic referents for medicine in European languages, what are obviously similar linguistic categories have a much broader *denotative* significance in most non-Western societies. The Kolongo-speaking Abron of the Ivory Coast, among whom I did medical anthropological research, are not untypical in this respect.

The word *sino*, which is best glossed as "medicine" in English, denotes agents used in the treatment and/or prevention of disease and includes countermagic against the malevolent, disease-producing action of others, as well as alternative (i.e., non-native) agents believed to be capable of maintaining or increasing wealth, physical strength, sexual prowess, and many other aspects of general well-being. In addition certain sino may be used against one's enemies to cause disease or ill fortune. For an Eng-

lish speaker the criteria which establish the boundaries for the function of sino might appear to be in
opposition. One set of these may be thought of as
the concept "restoration, maintenance or increase of
well being," which includes, but is not limited to, the
Western concept of health. This aspect of sino is
something like the *connotation* rather than the *deno-
tation* of health in English. The other set of criteria
relates to the use of sino as harmful rather than as
a curative agent. Let us not be tempted by the apparent disjunction of these two criteria. The concept of
sino as an aggressive force need not be interpreted
as contradictory or in opposition to its other use.

Power is used to promote the well-being of its
user, albeit sometimes at the expense of others. Seen
in this light the universe of all phenomena open to
the power of sino is conjunctive rather than disjunctive. Sino constitutes a class of substances (some
tangible, others intangible) which confer on the user
the power to restore, maintain, or increase the well-
being of himself or others. Some sino, including sino
used for countermagic, works at the expense of
others, while other sino is totally positive in its effect.
If some use of sino is considered evil, it is because
aggressive acts against members of one's own community are considered to be evil. Any disjunction
which exists lies not in the concept of sino but in
its use. The disjunction depends upon the concepts
of good and evil, as well as on the sense of community, and is social rather than linguistic. This is
made particularly clear by the fact that poison used
in the killing of game animals is also classed as sino.
It is a sino with a power against life, but because it

137

is used in a socially beneficial way it is good sino.

This is illustrated also, I think, by the use of poison ordeals in criminal trials, a custom which is widespread in Africa. Accused individuals are subjected to these ordeals but die only if they are culpable. The poison is believed to have no adverse effect on the innocent. In many languages the poisons used are classed as a member of the linguistic category which includes all medicines.

In addition to its use in the treatment of disease, sino provides an alternate set of means for the attainment of certain social ends. This set may be drawn upon by individuals to by-pass or overcome social and/or economic restrictions. Furthermore, the existence of such a set of alternatives within a behavioral system may be used as an ex post facto explanation for "unusual" social events or individual achievements. These metaphors and extended connotations associated with "medicine" provide a step in the connection between medical practice and other areas of behavior.

The diagnosed "causes" of sickness also reflect the extension of medicine into the social realm. Diagnosis is dependent upon symptoms, social circumstances, and the "insight" of the medicine man. Almost all behavioral systems include a set of causes in the class "that which produces disease." The most widely distributed of these are: (1) Natural causes; (2) breach of taboo or social regulation; (3) ancestor spirits; (4) ghosts; (5-6) witches and sorcerers; (7) various gods or other benevolent spirits; (8) malevolent spirits; (9) magic practiced by nonspecialists; (10)

soul loss. In some societies only a few of these agents are included in etiological theory, but only rarely are one or two of them taken as the sole agents responsible for disease. As we shall see in the next chapter, the Abron of the Ivory Coast include each of these categories in their disease theory.

Let us now discuss these categories and their relation to disease and the social system.

1. *Natural causes.* In primitive medicine although most belief systems exclude accidental death or natural disease, nonetheless certain minor conditions are taken as a matter of course and relegated to the role of nature. In addition, certain conditions are believed to be caused by some elements other than the personified supernatural. Nurge (1958) lists "indigestible foods, temperature changes, strong winds and vagrant breezes, vapor that arises from the ground when the sun comes out after a prolonged rain. Blood or air may be trapped in the body."

Latin American peasant medicine is full of references to cold and hot foods, an imbalance of which may cause illness. In addition, certain foods, depending upon their qualities, are said to be good or bad for specific disease conditions. These distinctions, and others such as those based on color found in French peasant medicine, can be traced back to Greek and Medieval medicine. Generally, references to the quality of food operate on the basis of either sympathetic magic in which the condition is imitated by some characteristic of the food, or on the basis of opposition, in which the food item, depending on its use and circumstance, brings the humors into or out of balance. Thus if one is suffering from "thick blood" green vegetables might be prescribed. In this case the red of blood is taken as the distinctive quality, and it is opposed by its complementary color.

The hot-cold distinctions are interesting also because they tend to be unsystematic throughout most of Latin America. Which foods are hot and which are cold is a matter of some dispute not only between communities but even within single villages. Categorization depends not upon innate quality but upon assumed effect upon physiological function.

Currier has suggested that the hot-cold syndrome is a model of social relations within the Mexican and Spanish American communities. "In this case, disease theory constitutes a symbolic system upon which social anxieties are projected, and it functions as a means of symbolically manipulating social relationships which are too difficult to manipulate on a conscious level in the real social universe." (Currier 1966:252)

This relationship is explained as follows:

In the process of weaning, the Mexican child is subjected to a prolonged period of acute rejection. As a result of this experience he forms strong subconscious associations between warmth and acceptance or intimacy on the one hand and between cold and rejection or withdrawal, on the other. In adult life these associations appear in those beliefs intimately concerned with the problem of personal security: theories about nourishment and about the prevention and cure of disease and injury. On a conscious level, then, the hot-cold syndrome is a basic principle of human physiology and it functions as a logical system for dealing with the problems of disorder and disease. On a subconscious level, however, the hot-cold syndrome is a model of social relations. (251-52)

140

2. *Breach of taboo or social regulation.* One of the major areas of social control mediated through medical theory comes from the belief that the breach of some culturally defined regulation will lead to disease or death. In Polynesia certain crops are taboo for parts of the year, thus conserving resources and spacing the consumption of certain food items. Among the Abron of the Ivory Coast yams cannot be taken from the garden until the harvest ceremony in the fall. Such a practice assures a long growing season and maximum yield. Customs of this type are referred to as first fruit ceremonies and are quite widely distributed among the world's peoples. The Abron also believe that the land cannot be farmed until sacrifice is made to it and that a day of rest must be observed or the land itself will punish the offending party.

Taboos on various types of food are so widespread as to make their documentation cumbersome. These occur in relation to social status (age ranking or sex distinctions or occupational distinctions), and often particular life crises are marked with specific food taboos. Pregnant women, for example, are often prescribed certain foods and forbidden others. In most cases the breaking of such restrictions results in disease. Elsewhere (Alland 1967) I have suggested that taboos and prescriptions for women during and after pregnancy may have medical effects on fertility and survival. My point was that in small-scale societies where survival is a major problem for the populations such customs would be expected to be medically positive while in large-scale or dense populations in which the carrying capacity of the environment might be threatened by further expansion such practices might prove to be less medically adaptive for the population at large. This set of hypotheses remains to be tested, but if it proves to be correct a new link will be established between medically related behavior and ecological adaptation.

The Netsilik Eskimos (Balikci 1963) believe that sickness is always caused by evil ghosts or by spirits usually angered by a breach of taboo. In the latter case the agent of disease is a supernatural entity, but the cause is the result of some violation of the rule system.

3. *Ancestor spirits.* Social groups in non-Western societies more often than not maintain continuity between the living and the dead. Thus, for example, a lineage in Africa (a corporate group consisting of relatives in either the male or the female line) usually includes a line of remembered ancestors who are considered to have right not only to certain categories of property but to ceremonial obeisance as well. Among the Abron regular sacrifice must be made to dead relatives who, if they are neglected, will punish the offending parties by bringing disease down upon them. The living communicate with the dead through the medium of sacrifice and ceremony; the dead communicate with the living by allowing life to continue in its orderly path or by creating disorder and disease. Such belief systems reinforce the maintenance of continuity within social groups.

In many societies, particularly in Africa, the demands ancestors make upon their living relatives are usually reasonable, but sometimes dead relatives may be a source of annoyance, anxiety, or even danger.

In such cases the living must protect themselves in various ways to ward off the attacks of unreasonable and capricious relatives who inhabit the world of the dead. An interesting example of the malevolent action of deceased relatives has been documented for the Dobuans by Fortune (1963):

In one Dobuan district there is a belief that the spirit of a person who has died with a swollen stomach is dangerous. It seeks to enter the body of another person, to cause him to die with a swollen stomach also. Infection with such a disease is due in the first place to a person going to a place where some time before he had killed a man or a woman. Everywhere Dobuan is spoken it is believed that if the killer returns to the place of the killed the blood of the killed will enter his body and swell it until he dies; and death with a swollen body is interpreted as having been caused so. But only among the Dobuans of one particular district is it believed that the spirit of a person so dying will enter the bodies of others still living and cause them to die also. . . . Such a spirit is obliged to enter and infect its next of kin only, the surviving members of its own *susu*. . . . But such a spirit, though it properly infects and enters one of its *susu* kin, is also believed to enter and infect anyone who owed the dead a debt and had not yet paid it by the time of the creditor dying. (Fortune 1963:179-80)

Such a belief suggests that the guilty act of an individual may come to rest upon an innocent relative. The kin tie in this case makes the next of kin somehow also open to punishment. The fact that the dead individual can also use a power which he has come by only through a criminal act to punish a non-relative who has wronged him reflects an interesting case of the extension of social control by the dead upon the living.

This case is limiting in the sense that the string of behavior which leads to the death of an innocent relative begins with an antisocial act on the part of the dead kinsman. There are also cases in which an ancestral spirit or other dead kinsman may kill or bring disease down upon members of his or her own family for malevolent reasons. Such beliefs reflect the ambivalent feelings which the living have for each other and for the ever-present spirits of the dead. The belief that the dead can cause disease provides an effective projective device in which ambivalent feelings among the living can be projected outward toward those who continue as members of the society only by virtue of the belief system. When such actions come from relatives and ancestors the belief would appear to reflect ambiguities and antagonisms which exist among the living members of the same kin group.

4. *Ghosts.* A separation is made here between ancestors and deceased relatives and the action of deceased non-kinsmen. These I shall call ghosts. Such a division has a heuristic function but is by no means universal. Among the Abron the soul of a dead individual is a complex of individual parts. One part is relatively benevolent, and it is to this part that sacrifice is made. Another part of the soul may become a ghost and attack either relative or stranger for no particular reason other than the bad intentions of the ghost itself. In many groups ancestors operate mainly as agents of social control while ghosts are seen as malevolent spirits who are responsible for much of

the evil and misfortune which befalls the living. When death, misfortune, and disease are brought about by the action of deceased nonkinsmen one would expect that this reflects social tensions within the society which are unrelated to kin-based antagonisms. Balikci writes of the Netsilik: ". . . evil ghosts were particularly dreaded. These were the wandering souls of men who died in bed believing they were killed by magic; they questioned the officiating shamans, accused neighbors and obviously feared death. No one feared the ghost of the hunter who met violent death." (1963:383)

5–6. *Witches and sorcerers.* I shall adhere to the distinction proposed by Evans-Pritchard (1937) between witches and sorcerers, although the same strictures placed on the distinction between ancestors and ghosts must apply here. A witch is an individual imbued with certain supernatural powers which may be used to inflict harm. While witches are capable of using medicines and magic they are semisupernatural creatures with such powers as the ability to transform themselves into animals, to make themselves invisible, and to fly. African witches like those of European folklore are generally also associated with a familiar, often a domestic animal. Sorcerers, however, are individuals with special knowledge, who may use this knowledge for good or evil. The status "witch" is hereditary and often involuntary. In some African tribes witches are evil in spite of their conscious intentions. Sorcerers, on the other hand, may learn their trade from other sorcerers.

In some societies both statuses exist; in others only one. As we shall see in the next chapter, the Abron make a rather clear distinction between the two categories. In most African societies, witches work for themselves and other witches, while sorcerers are for hire and practice their trade more or less openly. In many cases the status "witch" is empty in the sense that no one admits to being a witch although people believe in them.

The areas in which sorcery or witchcraft operate are many: weather, crops, a woman's fertility, or the luck of an individual, though it is in the realm of disease that most of their activity is focused. The extension of their powers beyond medical problems is not surprising since it merely follows the kind of extension we have already seen for medicine. Witches appear to function as outlets for hostility and aggression; as projective devices they turn antisocial feelings within the community outward towards "aliens" within their midst. They also offer a ready explanation for evil which befalls individuals. The belief in witchcraft also has a strong influence on social control. Individuals who act in some deviant fashion are likely to be branded as witches. In egalitarian societies individuals who amass too much wealth or prestige run the risk of being accused of practicing witchcraft (see Kluckhohn 1944).

What has been said of witches is also true for sorcerers. The magic which they control is a part of the technological system although in many cases, particularly when personal gain is involved, their activity is *sub rosa*. Although some sorcerers practice their trade openly they often work for others in secret. Illness may be explained as the result of witchcraft or sorcery, but there are cases in which the sorcerer may be appealed to to cure disease, particularly when the condition itself is thought to be caused by the actions of another sorcerer. Since sorcerers may act for good or evil, their status in the community is often ambiguous, and feeling towards them ambivalent.

7. *Various gods or other benevolent spirits.* The violation of taboo is usually punished by some supernatural entity. In some cases a taboo food has a spirit of its own which will punish the wrongdoer; in other cases it is the role of god or spirit to carry out the sanction. In addition gods may be used to explain misfortune and disease when it strikes the innocent. A favorite motto in Africa is "Man proposes, god disposes." In West Africa where the concept of a high god is widely distributed the apparently capricious actions of the supreme deity are often unexplainable in human terms. God is often blamed for misfortune when no other solution is possible. This is the existential deity of Kierkegaard or Kafka, whose plan is only partially revealed to man, or revealed in some distorted fashion, a reminder to man that he is clay and must live always at the feet of God.

8. *Malevolent spirits.* There are also supernatural forces, sometimes personified, which can produce only evil. They lurk in the wings ready to attack man. Much of the preventive medicine of non-Western peoples is directed against such creatures, and the combat is often seen as a mere stand-off. The belief in such creatures may have a great deal to do with the fact that most preventive medicine in the "emic" sense is nonrational. The belief in such supernatural beings is dysfunctional from the point of view of developing medical theory. Such was certainly the

case in Europe in the Middle Ages and beyond, and even today vestiges of these beliefs continue to make rational preventive medicine a difficult proposition among peasants. In the Middle Ages, latrines in Spain were often placed close to kitchens so that the stink of excrement would keep evil spirits out of the food! The persistence of such beliefs in folk systems suggests that their significance lies in areas outside of medicine.

10. *Magic practiced by nonspecialists.* While diseases are often believed to be caused by the supernatural or by such quasi-supernatural agents as witches and sorcerers, many behavioral systems have room for secular amateurs as well. In Africa, for example, the technique of object intrusion (sticking pins, nails, or other sharp objects into the image of an enemy) is widely known and may be practiced by anyone. In New Guinea and other areas of the Pacific, individuals may attack their enemies by performing magic over such items as hair, nail parings, fecal material, or the placenta of a victim. This kind of home medicine in reverse is another example of a "technological" system which contains alternate routes for the attainment of certain ends. The technology may be objectively useless, but it often accounts for events which appear to break the rule system as it is understood by the individuals living out their lives within the context of a particular behavioral system. It may also account for a good deal of psychosomatic disease, even death.

10. *Soul loss.* So far the categories of "cause" have all entailed entities external to the sick individual and acting in some way upon him, even if in some cases

disease results from self-initiated misdeeds. There are, however, many societies in which sickness may be the result of soul loss. The mind-body dichotomy in one form or another appears to be a common pre-occupation with human beings. The relative degree of attachment between the soul and the body varies from belief system to belief system. In our own tradition there is one soul which inhabits the body throughout life and can only be released from it at death. In other societies, the soul may leave the body, particularly at night. In some cases the wandering soul may decide it does not wish to return to the body; in other cases it may be captured by some spirit and taken away, as among the Eskimo. If the soul does not return, disease and finally death is the result. If health is to be maintained or restored the particular cause must be rooted out and the appropriate action taken.

There may be a relationship between the amount of esoteric knowledge in a medical system and the status of the medical practitioner. An esoteric system almost by definition increases the professional status of the native doctor and allows him to assert his influence, both directly and indirectly, in a rather large domain which we ourselves would consider to be extramedical. The prestige which the successful doctor achieves eases his role as a mediator of social relationships and makes his opinion on a variety of subjects valuable to the community at large. Such a situation is not lacking in American medicine, where the doctor commands respect from the layman not only in medical practice but well beyond it in the area of politics and even art. Doctors in general are a rather conservative group in American society. They have achieved a high status and are constantly guarding against the dilution of the position which they feel they have earned. The esoteric nature of the profession and the exclusive nature of the professional group reinforce the high status and allow for high reward as well. Medical doctors are jealous of their title and have at time objected to the use of the term in reference to holders of the Ph.D. even though the latter is a "higher," and was at one time a more prestigious, degree. On the other hand, quasi-professional medical personnel such as chiropracters have managed to achieve the title as well, much to the chagrin of a large number of medical doctors.

The extension of medical theory and the role of the therapist into nonmedical areas has other implications for the operation of behavioral systems, particularly in the area of ecological adjustments. The control which the shaman or therapist has over natural events and his responsibility for maintaining the well-being of his group may lead to an expansion of his role into the area of resource management, including power to make far-reaching decisions concerning the use of such resources. He may, for example, decide what the proper time for planting is, or when to harvest a particular crop. Such a role for the shaman is quite common, as among the Pueblo Indians of the Southwest United States. Balikci (1963) notes that among the Netsilik Eskimo:

Shamanistic control aims at maintaining a balance between people and environment usually in cases of disaster—

Shaman were asked where the game was. (1) Shaman could control thunder and put down snow storms. (2) Shaman could control individual or collective crises. (3) Numerous shamanistic acts and *ilisiniq* practices were meant to control interpersonal relations.

O. K. Moore (1957) has suggested in an extremely interesting paper that the process of divination, which is often the prerogative of the shaman, may have fundamental value for the maintenance of certain behavioral practices, particularly in economic behavior. Moore deals specifically with the case of scapulomancy among the Naskapi of Labrador. Moore suggests ". . . that some practices which have been classified as magic may well be directly efficacious as techniques for attaining the ends envisaged by their practitioners." (Moore 1957:69) He offers the hypothesis that scapulomancy randomizes the choice of hunting sites in such a way that animals are unable to learn from the hunters which areas of the forest are likely to be hunted. It is indeed a well-known feature of animal behavior that game animals do learn hunting patterns and thereafter tend to avoid dangerous areas.

It can be seen that divination based on the reading of cracks and spots, serves to break (or weaken) the causal nexus between final decisions about where to hunt and individual and group preferences in this matter. Without the intervention of this impersonal mechanism it seems reasonable to suppose that the outcome of past hunts would play a more important role in determining present strategy; it seems likely their selections of hunting routes would be patterned in a way related to recent successes

151

and failures. If it may be assumed that there is some interplay between the animals they seek and the hunts they undertake, such that the hunted and the hunters act and react to the other's actions and potential actions, then there may be a marked advantage in avoiding a fixed pattern in hunting. Unwitting regularities in behavior provide a basis for anticipatory responses." (Moore 1957:71)

Moore concludes:

Years ago Tylor noted that "the art of divination and games of chance are so similar in principle that the very same instrument passes from one use to the other." Tylor's observation is acute. However, it would appear that the relationship in "principle" is not between divination and games of chance, but between divination and games of strategy. It is only very recently that the distinction between games of chance and games of strategy has been drawn clearly . . . this theory makes evident how some classes of interactional problems can be solved optimally by means of a "mixed" or "statistical" strategy. In order to employ a statistical strategy it is necessary to have, adopt, or invent a suitable chance mechanism. Its being "suitable" is critical, for unless the chance device will generate appropriate odds for the problem at hand, then its potential advantage may be lost. It should go without saying that no one assumes that preliterate magicians are in any position to get the most out of their crude chancelike devices. Nevertheless, it is possible that through a long process of creative trial and error some societies have arrived at some approximate solutions for recurring problems. (73)

There is some evidence that belief systems, particularly that aspect concerning theories of disease etiology, may operate in some cases to reduce effectives stress and disease or to maintain an optimal man-land ratio, even though they are "objectively" nonempirical and based on false notions of causality.

Vayda (personal communication) has suggested that witchcraft accusations are the direct result of crowding and ensuing stress. An increase in witchcraft accusations leads to dispersal of population and reduction in stress. Vayda has extended this argument by suggesting that such dispersal may effectively redistribute populations over the land, so as to reduce the threat of environmental degradation. Dispersal would also have the effect of reducing the frequency of those epidemics which are dependent on density. It may be that in some cases an increased incidence of disease leads to an increase in witchcraft accusations (disease is the objective manifestation of witchcraft); this leads to dispersal, and dispersal leads to a lowering of disease incidence. This is a matter which demands closer examination. It is known that in some instances an increased incidence leads to dispersal and that in other cases groups tend to come together.

Among the Tiv (Bowen 1954) the occurrence of smallpox literally blows the society wide open; everyone flees from everyone else. At first glance one might suppose that such behavior does in fact lead to the spread of disease since the infecting agent may be carried over wide distances. This may be true in the case of smallpox, but it is possible that dispersal may have the reverse effect of reducing effective contact between sick and well individuals. In addition, demographic patterns such as dispersal or clumping

153

as a response to an increased incidence of disease may have different effects for different diseases.

From this flows the idea that the prevalent diseases in an area may have a selective effect on the development of the behavioral system, including religious beliefs. Thus while it has always been assumed by anthropologists that cognitive systems will effect the way in which environments are to be exploited, it may be that disease, among other environmental variables, acts as a selecting agent on both behaviors and beliefs. The prevalence of particular types of disease over others, and the frequency with which people become ill, for example, may have a profound effect on the shape of medical practice and on the ability of the practitioner to extend his influence into nonmedical aspects of society.

CHAPTER 7

MEDICAL SYSTEMS UNDER ACCULTURATION

Evolutionary change in somatic systems depends upon mutation; change in cultural systems depends upon innovation and borrowing (diffusion). Both types of change contain elements of randomness. Innovation may occur through accidental discovery, and contacts between populations are, at least partially, haphazard. The element of chance is increased to some extent when the unanticipated consequences of change throw a system off into some new and unexpected direction.

But to say that a culture trait arose through innovation or diffusion explains nothing. Certain traits diffuse well, others poorly. Certain populations are more amenable to change than others. Just as mutations occur within the context of somatic systems and environments, and draw their selective value from such contexts, cultural traits are affected by the existing behavioral system and the selective effects of the environment. Culturally based behavioral systems, as

155

systems, contain elements which restrict randomness to a degree unmatched in biological systems. Such restrictions depend upon the ability of human beings to think, to observe cause and effect relationships, and to construct theories which not only account for sets of phenomena but which also may be used to predict future results.

Good theories speed up the discovery process by reducing the random nature of the search. Such a reduction of randomness applies to both innovation and diffusion since new elements, no matter what their origin, must be worked into existing theories. I have already pointed out that "bad" theories may have the opposite effect, that is they may inhibit the discovery process. Thus I have suggested that where "bad" theories exist in a cultural domain random testing of the environment may be more effective in producing adaptive change than testing based on such theories. The reward value of a randomly discovered trait, however, may not be strong enough to overcome a negative theoretical set already existing within a cultural system. When this is the case a potentially advantageous trait may be rejected. In some instances, on the other hand, a new cultural element may lead to the rejection of existing theory.

With these restrictions in mind, it can still be said that the semi-isolation of human groups and the development of separate adaptive systems coupled with recontact among such groups should increase rates of change. The nonsomatic nature of cultural transmission allows groups to borrow from one another without concomitant interbreeding. New items of behavior can be adopted into, and adapted to, existing theories. The human species has the ability to remain a single biological unit and, at the same time, to occupy a wide range of environmental niches. This produces a reflexive effect in which ecological adjustments in one geographical zone may be rapidly transmitted to other zones where they maintain their adaptive value but in which they would be unlikely to originate. (See, for example, theories of urban development and the rise of civilization.) That is to say, innovations of a particular type may be more probable in certain environmental settings and in certain kinds of behavioral systems. In medicine, for example, advanced therapeutic techniques are most likely to develop in a "scientific climate," but they may then diffuse outward to less scientifically oriented populations, where they remain effective even when devoid of their theoretical implications. Furthermore the success of such traits may, under certain circumstances, lead to the development of a scientific orientation in the host population.

The process of change is influenced not only by the relationship between new elements and existing theories and the reward value of certain types of behavior, but also by similarities and differences between role systems in donor and receptor populations. When analogous roles exist in two different behavioral systems, change need only involve a shift in the content of existing roles. When no such analogues exist, change may require the adoption of an entirely new role or set of roles. What I am suggesting is that analogue roles act as templets for behavior and have the effect of facilitating and directing change. In this way the random nature of change in adaptive systems is further reduced.

Culture change through contact has been an ever-present element in the evolution of human behavioral systems. For the last several hundred years, and at an ever-increasing rate, Western culture, particularly technology, has provided the major impetus for change. This is certainly true for medicine, although various aspects of Western medicine are adopted into different alien societies at different rates. Frequently items of Western *materia medica* are more rapidly accepted than practitioners. Preventive medicine is, in general, the most difficult concept to introduce. This is consistent with the hypothesis that much of what we would define as preventive medicine lies outside of indigenous medical theory. In many cases what Westerners might define as rational preventive measures will be considered irrelevant by local peoples. In addition, since the introduction of rational preventive medical techniques must crosscut many areas of behavior, ranging from such items as ritual and the formalities of social relationships to economic activity, they may be resisted because their acceptance would produce severe disruptions in areas of behavior which lie beyond medical theory and practice.

In this chapter I shall describe the medical system of the Abron of the Ivory Coast and discuss its relationship to problems of culture change as they affect the introduction of Western medicine. It is my conviction that the model presented can be extended cross culturally to account in part for the relative facility with which medical change can be introduced into a foreign setting. The line of attack presented here depends upon role theory, specifically what I have referred to as behavioral templets. It must be stressed, however, that the acceptance or rejection of specific medical practices will also depend upon the existence in native systems of techniques of medication and therapy analogous to Western medicine and upon those isomorphisms which may exist between native disease theory and scientific medicine. Finally, acceptance or rejection will be strongly influenced by the design of any particular demonstration project. Such factors as cost (minimax relationships), the overall effect on nonmedical aspects of behavior, and the type of personnel involved (age, sex, social standing, ethnic identification) will all play an important role in the final outcome of the contact situation. These factors are all related to the process of internal adaptation discussed in Chapter 2.

Rosman (1962), realizing that it is individuals who acculturate and not cultures, has suggested that change is routed through particular status positions, and that individuals playing specific roles are likely to acculturate at different rates.

Borrowing from Goffman (1959), Rosman has also investigated the concept of self-image in role playing and has related it to the specific context of social change. In his analysis of culture change among the Kanuri of Northern Nigeria, Rosman focused upon status positions within the host culture.

The discussion here shall be extended to the images members of a host culture form of outsiders playing new and often ambiguous roles in the contact situation. The point is a simple one: No matter what kind of face an actor may wish to present to strangers, the image he projects will be determined in part by the preconceived notions of the audience. These notions will center around the role system of the host culture. When the new role has an analogue in the host culture, the image formed will be found in this analogue, and the actor will be pegged into a previously existing part. This can create considerable difficulties for agents of social change, but it also serves to preserve, at least for a time, the existing role system. These analogue roles must be analyzed in terms of structure, that is, the network of social relationships within a society, and in terms of the cognitive map associated with behavior, affect, and beliefs imbedded in the role system. I will attempt to illustrate my argument with data gathered in the course of field work among the Abron of the Ivory Coast. Three contact roles will be dealt with, that of secular medical doctor, the trained nurse, and the missionary doctor—and their analogies in Abron culture, the *sise* or curer, and the *kparese* or priest-doctor. Obviously the cultural context of these roles lies in the area of disease theory, diagnostics, and treatment.

As among so many preliterate people, there is no place for natural death in the Abron belief system. People sicken and die because some power, good or evil, has acted against them. The forces which cause sickness and death vary in power, motivation, and technique. Some may kill without warning; others kill slowly so that counter practices may be instituted against them; some do not wish to kill. Disease symptoms are a sign that something must be done to return the patient to a state of well-being. For an effective cure, the underlying cause of a disease must be discovered and treated along with the significant symptoms.

Abron disease theory contains a host of agents which may be responsible for a specific condition, each of them associated with a set of possible reasons for spreading sickness. These agents cut across the natural and supernatural world. Ordinary people —equipped with the proper technical skills—sorcerers, various supernatural entities—such as ghosts, bush devils, and witches—or the supreme god *Nyame*, acting alone or through lesser gods, may all cause disease.

Gods (*gbawkaw*) usually make people sick when they have not been treated with the required reverence. People who neglect their ceremonial duties are a prime target for illness. Ghosts (*puni*) also cause illness when they are neglected in ceremony, but they also kill if they are lonely in heaven (*punu*) and seek the company of a particular relative. Bush devils (*bonzam*) are malevolent creatures which stalk the savannah ready to pounce on any unsuspecting person who wanders by. If an individual attacked by a bonzam manages to return to the village, he is usually overtaken with insanity. Sorcerers, usually Moslems, hire themselves out to individuals who wish to attack an enemy. They are often employed to make a rival in love impotent. *Obypi* or dead penis is a frequent complaint of Abron men, and even those who have fathered a considerable family claim to have been victims of this disease at one time or another during their sexual careers. Witches (deresogo) act out of personal jealousy and work only for themselves or other witches. The status "witch" is an empty category as far as real individuals are concerned. It is filled through the projection of aggressive motives onto semisupernatural individuals believed to live in the community of men.

Witches, sorcerers, and those who are brave enough to attempt black magic on their own through the use of object intrusion face the constant danger that their efforts may be turned against them. Priests, sorcerers, and even some secular curers sell medicine which protects a person against the attacks of others. If an individual attempts to kill someone possessing effective countermagic, he himself will die. A priest who moved to the village where I lived during field work told me that a witch had tried to kill her. Her own magic was ineffective against this particular witch, but another priest promised to help her. She was told that if she left her own village and used the medicine which she had been given, the witch would die in its next attempt on her life. One week after she moved to my village her uncle died. He was taken by all concerned to have been the witch responsible for the woman's original illness.

A schizophrenic woman of another village is said to have become insane when her attempts to kill her brother had failed. Her disease was related to her brother's countermagic. The difference between magic and countermagic is that magic can be brought into play at any time while countermagic is effective only when a person attempts to bewitch its owner. As the Abron have strong sanctions against any forms of aggression, countermagic is a preferred protective technique. When it is used a person is killed by his own perfidity, not by the action of another, since he dies only when he brings his own evil into play. The guilt is his own and the "real victim" is left with a clear conscience.

While cause is the most important diagnostic item in the eventual treatment of disease, symptoms are also treated. These are grouped into various named categories, and the Abron have a rather elaborate taxonomy for illness. Symptoms occasionally provide clues to the causative agent (chest pains, for example, are often said to be the result of object-intrusion magic), and there is a range of specific treatments for disease categories. Many of these are herbal and many also, no doubt, are effective in therapy. Kerharo and Bouquet (1950) list a considerable number of drug plants used by the Abron.

With such a wide variety of cause and an elaborate diagnostic category system, it is not surprising that the Abron also avail themselves of multiple treatment sources. These may be grouped as follows:

Self-care. If a person is only mildly ill and familiar with the treatment for a condition which is not considered serious, he will usually treat himself (in spite of the fact that all disease is theoretically caused by some agent which must be identified and dealt with). Most Abron are familiar with medication for diarrhea and are particularly fond of applying self-therapy with potassium permanganate enemas. Superficial scratches are covered with leaves and forgotten until they develop into infections, as they so often do. Mild fevers are treated with a variety of widely known

163

herbs. When sickness occurs, the affected individual will usually wait some days before seeking help from a specialist but, if the condition persists, such aid will eventually be sought. Because symptoms are treatable as entities separate from the cause of disease, individuals with what are considered mild conditions may purchase drugs either from Moslem merchants or from traders in the markets who sell a variety of Western medicines.

Nonprofessional curer. When a sick person has not been able to obtain relief after several days of mildly annoying illness, he will usually seek out a villager known to be familiar with various medicinal herbs. These practitioners do not charge for their services, although they generally receive a gift if a cure results from their treatment. Such curers are symptom-oriented and are usually familiar with several alternate forms of medication for specific conditions. Medical knowledge of this type is picked up casually from priests, Moslems, Europeans, and other Africans. A native who has been cured through European medication might recommend the same treatment to a sick friend with an entirely different ailment.

Some of the medicines used by these therapists are purely magical, consisting of charms and concoctions which could by no stretch of the imagination have any but psychological therapeutic value; others are probably efficient cures. Treatment for any eye condition in infants, for example, consists of painting the eyebrows of the child with white and brown clay. No medication is applied directly to the eye. On the other hand, many of the local drug plants function well as vermifuges, analgesics, and fever depressants. No distinction is made in Kolongo (the language of the Abron) between nonmedical protective devices, such as charms, and real medicine. Both categories are classed as *sino*.

The priest or kparese. If a person is very ill, sick for a prolonged period, or is convinced that something or someone is trying to kill him, he will seek the aid of a kparese (pl. *kparesogo*). Ideally, kparesogo are consulted for any illness, but a sick individual who feels little anxiety about a condition known to be mild and nonfatal rarely bothers.

Conditions with severe internal symptomology (violent headache, stomach ache, high fever, or extreme weakness) are usually signs which lead the patient to the kparese. While most kparesogo are familiar with a large selection of medicinal plants, they concern themselves more with disease agents. Their main job is to find the cause of illness. To do this, they must consult their personal deity (gbawkaw), who will determine why a person is ill and also prescribe treatment. If the kparese decides that a person is being attacked by a witch, he will fight the patient's tormentor and, at the same time, either prescribe medication for the symptoms or refer the patient to another specialist for medicine. This procedure will be followed in most cases of illness which are attributed to any form of black magic. When a person has become sick through the neglect of ritual duties, the kparese will attempt to set things straight by instructing the sick person in the necessary propitiatory ritual. In such cases the kparese will again treat the symptoms or refer the patient to a specialist.

Since kparese are familiar with known drugs, and

165

because they sometimes treat symptoms as well as causes, one would suppose that their treatment of disease entities would differ little from that of other curers. However, this is not always so. A kparese will rely on his or her gbawkaw for diagnosis to such an extent that the patient's symptoms will cease to function as information cues in the diagnostic process. It is not uncommon, therefore, for a kparese to ignore his patient's physical complaints. If a kparese were to devote too much attention to symptoms and ask his patient too many questions, the power of his gbawkaw would come under suspicion. Thus treatment by a kparese is very much like the comic situation in Western culture in which a patient refuses to tell the doctor his symptoms, because it is the doctor's job to determine what is wrong. Medication prescribed by kparesogo for specific conditions is often wide of the mark. This may explain (at least partially) why kparesogo often send their clients to specialists for treatment of symptoms.

Kparesogo make their reputations on the number of cures they perform, their ability to predict the future, and their ability to ward off epidemics. Their role of diviner serves them well, since they can predict an epidemic where there is none in the offing, and then claim to have warded it off through the operation of preventive magic.

During the course of this study, a kparese who had moved to the village where I lived performed a rite of divination shortly after her arrival. During the ceremony she predicted an epidemic, but promised to ward it off if she could obtain the cooperation of the villagers. This was forthcoming, and the disease

166

never appeared, much to the relief of the grateful villagers. The new kparese had established herself in the hearts of the people, and her business prospered thereafter.

If, in spite of a kparese's efforts, a patient dies, the failure is blamed on some evil power, lack of attention on the part of the patient to required ritual, or inefficient medication prescribed by some outside source. Kparesogo themselves are rarely, if ever, held responsible for failure in treatment.

Training for the role of kparese begins early in a candidate's life. Relatives of kparese, particularly children or grandchildren, and occasionally a non-relative, are apprenticed to a kparese who trains them in divination, magic, medical practice, and religious ritual. Until he or she graduates, often by inheriting the master's gbawkaw, the apprentice functions as an assistant to the kparese. Only the better known kparesogo have apprentices, and even they have only one, since it is felt that their power must be passed on to a single individual.

Secular curer (sise). Sisogo stand half way between the nonprofessional curer and the kparese. The amount of attention paid to symptoms by sisogo reflects this position. While they concentrate on treating specific conditions and are familiar with native drug plants, sisogo tend toward magical practice more than secular curers. Many sisogo prepare countermagic as well as charms, and some consult their gbawkaw. None of them, however, are diviners, nor are they employed to combat directly the effects of ghosts, witches, or evil spirits.

Another important distinction between sisogo and

167

secular curers is the fact that sisogo like kparesogo are trained for their positions, although not as rigorously as priests.

None of these status positions in Abron society are full-time occupations, but sisogo and kparesogo who are well known and successful devote a good deal of their time to professional practice. Like the kparese the reputation of the sise depends upon success. Those who have built up good reputations are used by kparesogo for referrals in the same way that Western doctors use specialists as referrals for their patients. The relationship between kparesogo and sisogo is amiable because they complement each other's functions and do not compete directly for patients the way, for example, doctors and osteopaths might in our culture.

Moslems (sogo). The Abron have an ambivalent attitude toward the Moslem curers because their reputations are based primarily on sorcery. Most of my informants stated flatly that they would not consult a sogo in case of illness. The attitude of many was that Moslems sometimes make people sick in order to be hired later as therapists. If a man becomes impotent, he may seek out the particular sogo he feels is responsible and pay what amounts to a blackmail fee. He may also go to another Moslem in the hope that sickness brought about by one sogo can best be cured by another. The general dislike of sogo as medicine men does not stop the Abron from buying charms from Moslem traders in the market place. The favorite item in this vein are rings, bracelets, bits of minerals, old beads, and parts of animals, such as skulls and snake skins; however, as a rule,

168

these charms can only be made effective if they are activated by the blessings of a kparese. The Moslem is a trader who sells potential medicines which must be activated by an indigenous religiomedical practitioner.

Some non-Moslem Abron also believe in the power of the Koranic charms which all Moslems wear. These are often bought from sogo and are considered by some to be effective without further benediction. It is obvious that sogo are trusted more as bearers of preventive medicine than as curers in cases of illness. Their role as practitioners of black magic disturbs their possible function as therapists.

WESTERN THERAPISTS AND WESTERN MEDICINE

The Abron have had experience with Western medicine for at least thirty years. A Catholic mission located in the center of Abron territory has served the area through its maternity hospital, and the government operates several clinics as well as a hospital in the region.

If there is a clinic in a particular village, the local inhabitants are likely to seek medical aid there. Otherwise, they will go to the nearest native treatment source (kparese, sise, or secular curer, depending on what they think is wrong with them). The less accessible the hospital, the less likely is it to be used, since the Abron will usually not go out of their way to seek treatment by Europeans. The hospital is a strange place, often staffed by non-Abron, and people are afraid to stay there for prolonged periods. When patients do come they usually bring some of their family to keep them company. Surgery, which is not a part of Abron medicine, creates the fear that European doctors sometimes maim their patients. This fear is occasionally borne out by necessary amputations. Furthermore, the system of free medication is abused by a few unscrupulous nurses who charge patients for medication, or attempt to sell them special medicines which they say are not given to nonpaying patients.

The Abron respect the value of European medicine and often request aid from nonmedical personnel, such as lay missionaries and traders. While certain medical techniques have gained a special reputation among the people (women have become particularly willing to consult the maternity clinics, which are run by both the missions and the government), confidence in Western drugs seems greater than confidence in doctors. This is reinforced by many factors. The majority of patients in the clinic and hospital are examined only casually by African nurses, and only the most serious cases are referred to the overworked doctors. Most clinics are staffed exclusively by nurses and even lesser technicians, who often prescribe medication when they ought to refer the patient to the hospital with a doctor in residence. There is little ritual associated with Western medical treatment. The paraphernalia of the examination room is seldom seen, and medical examinations are usually cursory; thus the doctor often appears to be an unnecessary adjunct to the distribution of medicine.

170

Shortly after World War II antibiotics became popular in the area. Today, they have become incorporated into folk medicine and are used at random for a variety of conditions; they are also a form of preventive medicine. The hypodermic injection has won particular public admiration. Abron going to the clinic for treatment feel slighted if do not receive their *"picure."* In most cases their desire is satisfied, since the general approach to medicine in the area is to use a liberal supply of antibiotics by injection in what is known as "shotgun treatment." This practice may be defended on the grounds that medical facilities are understaffed and overworked, but it has led the people to believe that there are certain standard key cures for all illnesses.

Furthermore, it is not difficult to procure even the most dangerous drugs. Although it is illegal in the Ivory Coast to purchase most drugs without a prescription, almost any of them may be bought on the native market or over the counter in trading-center drug stores. Penicillin tablets are sold in every village, and even such drugs as streptomycin and cortisone appear from time to time. In addition to the fact mentioned previously, that Africans tell their friends about medicines which have made them well, patients are often given empty serum tubes after their treatment, and it is therefore not difficult for them to become familiar with the names of various drugs. One villager approached me for advice on a certain medicine which had been recommended to him by a friend as a general tonic and cure-all. He produced a bottle of pills which, on examination, turned out to be female hormones. Another villager

171

requested that some streptomycin be obtained for him; he also showed the bottle with a label he could not read.

The Abron show great interest in obtaining medicines which can make them strong or protect them against snakes, scorpions, gunshot wounds, and real or imagined enemies. They believe that Europeans can supply these and other even more magical products, and they are often willing to pay large sums for them. Americans have a particularly strong reputation for possessing such "medicine." Many Africans of the West Coast are familiar with the catalogues of various companies advertising merchandise imbued with supernatural power.

I was pestered for such items as rings which would make the owner rich, good at boxing, a paramour, or protect him against evil magic; wallets which accumulate wealth by themselves if placed under the owers pillows at night; and various potions which improve the looks or strength of the wearer. An American giving a ring to an Abron will invariable be asked what powers it has. Catholic, Moslem, and pagan Abron share these beliefs with equal intensity, and it is unlikely that missionary efforts will do much to erode them in the near future. The American missionaries located about twelve miles from the village in which this author worked are so vexed by the problem of magic that they no longer wear their wedding rings. Since all these items are glossed in the language with medicine (sino), it is difficult to convince the Abron that medication dispensed by the hospital or clinic is different in kind from the magical items advertised in pulp magazines.

172

As far as they are concerned, magic and medicine of this type make up a subclass of sino unique only in that their original source is European or American. The uncontrolled use of drugs is further enchanced by the belief that drugs are, or should be, in the public domain, to be used at the patient's own risk. Sacred medical knowledge, the concern of the kparese, is restricted to the element of supernatural combat, which is only one element in Abron disease theory.

THE WESTERN DOCTOR

Two types of trained doctor are found in the Ivory Coast; one is the so-called *médecin africain*, and the other is the fully accredited doctor. The former are Africans who have been schooled in a special two-year course in medicine at the University of Dakar, the latter have received the full course of medical training in a European university. The category médecin africain is the result of two factors. One is certainly the great shortage of medical personnel in French Africa and the consequent need to train competent practitioners in the least possible time. Second, there is little doubt that the French did not want Africans to hold medical degrees equal to those held by their own doctors. As far as the French are concerned, the médecin africain has inferior status and is limited in his practice to the treatment of Africans. This is reflected in the fact that the term applied in France to medical doctors, médecin, is reserved for the médecin africain. French doctors are always referred to as *docteur* in Africa. For Ivoirians, on the other hand, there is no distinction between European- and African-trained doctors. What is important to them is access to European-style treatment and, more often than not, this means European drugs. The doctor and his hospital are a source of such medication. In the eyes of the Abron, the doctor is equivalent to the sise, but he has great knowledge of and, no less important, control over a vast storehouse of powerful medicine. In one sense he is the *primus inter pares* of the sisogo.

The kparesogo themselves see European and African doctors in this light, and they frequently refer their own patients to the hospital or clinic for treatment. If the patient recovers, the kparese gets the credit for removing or placating the cause of illness. The doctor gets the credit for treating the symptoms. The way in which the doctor plays his role supports this identification. In examination he is symtom-oriented, his treatments apply to the disease itself, and, when this is cured, the doctor is satisfied. The doctor does not pray over his patients, he does not foretell the future, and he is unable to prescribe ritual behavior.

There are also certain disadvantages to European medication. When treatment at the hospital or clinic requires long periods of therapy for success, the Abron usually tire of it and go back to the sise or kparese. This situation does not arise in native medicine, since the Abron system is based on power and counterpower, which must constantly be manipulated in an attempt to find the proper combination for cure. Lack of success in medication signifies the need for further divination. Since Europeans do not function as diviners, natives leave them for indigenous practitioners. When this happens, psychosomatic factors may come into play, and there may be significant remission of symptoms in a large enough proportion to reinforce the belief in African medicine.

THE NURSE

While it is obvious that the doctor does not threaten the kparese, he certainly does pose a threat to the sise. But he is not alone in this respect, since he is not the exclusive source of Western medicine. The trained nurse, who is also called "doctor" by the Abron and who has more contact with patients than real doctors, is an important source of medication.

Nurses assigned to the clinic or hospital are trained in general nursing practice—simple diagnosis, drug prescription, and hypodermic techniques. Other nurses are stationed in villages around the territory. These are special personnel trained only in the diagnosis and treatment of a single epidemic or endemic disease (sleeping sickness and malaria are two examples). The villager soon learns that these nurses are useless for general medication. During a meningitis epidemic in the north just above Abron country one such nurse was found cringing in his hut, afraid (for good reason) to make his usual rounds. He was equipped to treat malaria and was unable to cope with the epidemic at hand.

The fact that the Abron class nurses with doctors under the latter term reduces their overall confidence in the ability of Western-trained personnel to treat disease effectively. Sisogo attempt to maintain their position from the competition of the doctor-nurse-sise by exploiting the belief held by many that African medicine is better for some conditions than is Western medicine, and by relying more heavily on magical devices. But even here they are trapped by the fact that Western sino includes such devices, at least as far as most Abron are concerned.

THE MISSIONARY DOCTOR

The missionary doctor is in a unique and, for him, peculiar position. He is, in a very real sense, a kparese in spite of himself. His behavior fits much more closely than that of the secular doctor the established role content of the kparese. He is concerned with both the religious and biological aspects of disease and, as far as the Abron are concerned, treats cause (sin) as well as symptoms. So far there are only Catholic missionary medical personnel in Abron country, but I have no doubts that Protestant missionary doctors will fit the kparese role equally well.

The position of the kparese is of course threatened by any missionary on purely religious grounds, but the medical missionary is more dangerous in this respect than his lay brother because the major part of the kparese's activity is related to the prevention and treatment of disease. Healthy Abron are often willing to listen to Christian teaching, but when sickness strikes they return to their own treatment sources. The medical missionary fights the kparese on his own ground; he does not need to refer his flock to outside medical resources. It is for this reason that hostility to medical missionaries is more intense among kparesogo than toward the lay preacher or the secular doctor. The preacher is generally considered relatively ineffective, and the doctor as a sise is actually an ally in the fight against disease.

The missionary doctor has an advantage over the secular doctor in converting the Abron to a belief in Western medicine because his status position has a positive and powerful analogue within the Abron social system. The Abron consult the missionary doctor not only to receive medication but also to protect themselves from supernatural enemies which persist even after an individual converts to Christianity. The missionary doctor, because he is like a kparese, protect the community from evil. Catholic and pagan Abron alike believe that a witch entering the door of the missionary hospital is a dead witch. When the missionary claims that there are no such things as witches he is met with a knowing shrug. No one likes to talk about witches but everyone knows that they exist.

SUMMARY

Those aspects of social structure and the cognitive system which affect the status positions of Western medical personnel in Abron culture may be summarized in the following way:

1. The semantic class sino includes magical devices and real medicine, either of which may be

native or Western. This fact tends to minimize the role of the doctor in the control and distribution of sino. Many items of this class which are highly valued are obtainable only from other than medical sources.

2. The fact that nurses and doctors are included in the semantic class "doctor" (I refer to the English loan word in Kolongo) further dilutes the doctor role in the eyes of his Abron patient.

3. The Western approach to medical practice is most like the approach of the sise in Abron culture. Secular medical personnel are therefore at least partially equated with their analogue, the sise. As such they function as adjuncts to the priest-doctors or kparesogo.

4. The missionary doctor, on the other hand, because he practices medicine and performs religious ritual, is classed with the analogue role kparese. While the secular doctor presents no threat to the kparese, and is in fact exploited by him, the missionary doctor is in a position to supplant the kparese in medical practice. This may lead to active hostility between missionary and priest (a conflict the missionary welcomes).

5. The status kparese is more strategic within the Abron social system than the status sise. This is true because the role of the kparese extends to the entire religious life of the Abron, and the sise is merely one alternative source of medication. The author would surmise, therefore, that the missionary doctor will have much greater success in the long run in the introduction of Western medical practice in Abron culture.

CHAPTER 8

CONCLUSION

In this book I have tried to suggest ways in which the material and techniques of medical anthropology can be used to investigate the process of human biological and cultural adaptation. The theoretical orientation has been that of biological evolution. Such a theory attempts to explain the processes by which populations adapt to their environments. Evolution involves the development of stable systems which are maintained through negative feedback. Stability in systems reflects the conservative force of adaptation in which systems which have become well adjusted to their environments tend to maintain themselves through time. But change is also a constant feature of evolution, and no system is ever completely stable. Through the process of environmental selection and positive feedback random change is sifted out in the direction of maximization, that is, in the direction of better self-regulating systems. New features of a system which increase maximization are selected for, while those which decrease maximization are selected against. What this means is: (1) that populations carrying more efficient systems replace or absorb populations carrying less efficient systems if such groups are competing for the same environment and (2) that traits within systems which increase efficiency come to replace less efficient traits. The mechanisms which produce change are of two types (1) somatic and (2) cultural.

I have suggested that the proper measure of adaptation is population increase but that such increase must be tied to the carrying capacity of the environment. This is necessary simply because in the long run population increase without a concomitant increase in carrying capacity will inevitably lead to a degradation of the environment, which in turn will reduce the size of the population. An increase in the carrying capacity of the environment means that the population exploiting that environment has increased its ability to extract calories and other essential nutrients from that environment without degrading it. The outcome of such a process is the conversion of such nutrients into organisms.

One of the essential problems in evolutionary studies is the proper measure of carrying capacity. The measures used cannot be applied universally to all populations and all environmental settings. Local environmental and technological factors must be analyzed to project the total number of human beings such an environment can support under such a technological system without risk of degradation. This is not a simple problem, and much research remains to be done both for the development of effective measures and for comparisons between actual populations and projected carrying capacities.

While archaeological and physiographic evidence suggests that human populations have degraded their environments in the past, modern estimates of carrying capacity suggest that contemporary primitive human populations do not approach their optimal number (Marshall Sahlins, personal communication). If this is the case, reasonable explanations for these results must be derived and tested. In addition, we need more evidence concerning the ways in which carrying capacity can be altered through changes in technology and social systems. (Julian Steward in particular has made an important contribution in this area, especially in his studies of the organization of work.) We need to know more about the relationships which must exist between technological systems, work patterns, and health and disease. It is frequently the case among primitive and peasant populations that much of the energy extracted from the environment by humans is lost to internal parasites. The amount of blood lost each year in the United States because of hookworms is truly appalling, but it does not even begin to compare with the effect of bilharzia (schistosomiasis) on the population of Egypt, where the infestation rate is about 95 per cent of the peasant population. Around the world poor health due to infectious disease or poor nutritional status is responsible for a tremendous waste of resources.

Human adaptation involves the twin problems of economic and medical adjustment. These are intertwined because the technological sphere has direct and indirect effects upon health and disease rates. In addition, improvements in the health standards of a population may effect the techno-environmental balance through increases in population.

Health and disease are major concerns for all humans. It is no surprise therefore that medical practice frequently comes to occupy a central place in human behavioral systems. The role of the medical practitioner often becomes amplified through the generalization of his powers to social and economic problems. Control over death, no matter how imperfect, places the medical practitioner in a position of power over other aspects of the supernatural realm. The supernatural is manifested in the real world through disease, natural disaster, and changes in environmental parameters. When these are taken as a single area of concern, the doctor can easily extend his authority into the areas of resource management and social control. Medical practice may be used to reduce social tensions, produce alternate explanations for unusual phenomena, and help to maintain environmental adjustments through the reinforcement of taboo. I have suggested as an hypothesis that the type of diseases present in a population and their relative frequency should affect not only the development of medical practice but also the effectiveness of the practitioner in extending his powers of control into nonmedical areas. In addition, the degree to which the medical practitioner has exclusive control over medical information may effect his power to manipulate individuals.

The general epidemiological pattern of a population may have a selective effect on the development of such projective systems as religion. A high incidence of disease might be connected with malevolent supernatural entities, for example. It is unfortunate that little attention has been paid by anthropologists to the effects of ecological conditions, particularly disease, on belief systems.

Since many medical practitioners and folk medical theories operate in spheres which extend beyond disease, the effectiveness of medical practice and theory as an adaptive device must be judged not only in terms of disease control, but also in terms of its overall contribution to adaptive patterns. This raises a host of difficulties because it extends medical anthropological research beyond the realm of specifically medical problems. One of the major difficulties involves measurement and the specification of cause. How do we know which traits contribute to the maximization or stability of a behavioral system? How do we measure the effects of these traits once they have been dissected out of the behavioral system?

One aspect of this problem has been attacked by Paul Collins and Andrew P. Vayda in their approach to functional analysis (see Collins 1965, Vayda and Rappaport 1968). These authors consider the proper task of functional analysis to be the demonstration of self-regulating systems. In such systems there exists a variable (R) which must be maintained within tolerable limits in order for the system to persist through time. The maintenance of the R variable is threatened by changes in environmental parameters. The R variable is kept within its acceptable range through changes in s, or supporting variables. If one is to test this notion, it becomes necessary to define

183

a system, to state the R variable and its tolerable range, and to measure changes in s variables as they respond to environmental variations. Vayda has suggested that the potlatch ceremony of the Northwest Coast Indians operates to maintain environmental balance, in this case distribution of resources, among various social segments of the various tribes. In terms of medical problems, the incidence of disease and the category of diagnosis offered by the medical practitioner may be related to such types of regulation. Social diagnosis, that is where cause is attributed to certain social groups, may vary according to fluctuations in environmental parameters, for example, shortages of particular nutrients or density of population. A variation in frequency and type of psychosomatic disorder encountered in populations may also be linked to changes in social tensions which are themselves influenced by environmental parameters.

The problems inherent in the investigation of positive feedback are more difficult. Several suggestions have been made throughout this book. One of these, which I consider central to the problem of adaptation, is the analysis of minimax strategies in which behavior which produces economic gain is balanced against hazards to health generated either directly or indirectly by such behavior. The first question is: Under what conditions do such hazardous behaviors develop? The second question is: What modifications in these behavioral patterns occur which make them safer for the populations involved?

In addition, I have suggested that problems of health and disease be investigated in terms of our own knowledge of public health practices. The method here involves a detailed ecological and medical survey of particular populations with the construction of some kind of disease scale for that area. This is not an easy problem, however, for while one might explain the incidence of a specific disease by recourse to behavior, it will be difficult to predict what diseases *might* occur in an area if the behavior were different. The major way around this difficulty, as I see it, and the solution is by no means perfect, is to choose field situations in which several ethnic groups inhabit the same ecological zone. The behavioral systems and methods of economic exploitation of such groups will differ. The epidemiological patterns characteristic of each group can be expected to differ as well, hopefully, at least in part, according to variables imbedded in the behavioral system.

There is no dearth of geographic areas which meet these requirements. The relationship between caste membership and disease in various regions of India is open for investigation, and there are several regions of Africa in which divergent ethnic groups live in the same macro-niche. Within a small relatively homogeneous segment of the Ivory Coast near the Ghana and upper Volta borders, for example, one finds separate populations: one dependent upon cattle, another upon yams, and a third upon millet. Settlement patterns, religious practices, and social systems among these groups differ. Furthermore, two of them are ethnically related, belonging to the same language family, while the third is unrelated. Two of these groups appear to have been in the area for a considerable period of time; the third is a relative newcomer. What I am suggesting here is a kind of

CONCLUSION

cross cultural field research in which the natural environmental parameters are held as constant as possible while behavioral and medical differences are investigated.

In addition to field research, the development of adaptation to disease may be investigated through the methods of historical epidemiology as outlined in Chapter 4.

This book also contains a series of specific hypotheses which relate to the evolutionary model presented in Chapter 2. One of my major concerns has been an analysis of the development of strategies through which adaptation to environment occurs. Such strategies must represent compromises between problems of internal adaptation and external adaptation, and between profit and loss where medical and economic problems intersect. I have suggested that strategies develop through a process in which the environment is tested. Such testing may be conscious or unconscious, relatively random or directed through the application of some theory. Logically one should expect good theories to speed effective adaptation and poor theories to inhibit successful change (but not all change). A correlate to this is that an open process of trial and error not tied to theory should be more effective in the development of adaptation than experiments tied to poor theory.

In line with the above argument I have suggested that preventive medicine as we would define it (that is practices isomorphic with known principles of public health in Western medicine) should be more effective than therapeutic techniques in most if not all primitive societies. This hypothetical effectiveness is related to the suggested *lack* of connection between medical theory and good health practices.

Adaptation depends upon positive feedback from the environment. Such feedbacks may be slow or rapid, depending on the degree of ambiguity in the sources of information. The less noisy a system, the more likely that useful information can be extracted from it. The development of successful cures for purely physical illness is inhibited by extremely noisy sources of information. Patients tend to get well with or without effective therapy, and the experimenter must discover empirical links between specific chemical products and disease. On the other hand, cures for psychosomatic illness develop directly out of reactions on the part of the patient to what the practitioner does rather than what his medicine does. (The system is therefore less noisy.) The fact that the behavior of medical personnel in many widely distributed populations is similar in so many respects suggests that feedbacks for the development of psychosomatic cures have been effectively exploited.

I have suggested that discovery procedures are influenced not only by feedback relationships, and the type of theory present, but also by similarities and differences in role systems between cultures in contact. Thus where analogue roles exist, change will tend to be directed through such roles. In addition, items associated with such roles (specific practices and behavioral affect) will tend to be reinterpreted in the light of the traditional rules for acting out these roles.

In sum, I have attempted to present a coherent

CONCLUSION

theory of human behavioral adaptation and to con-
nect such a theory to medically oriented behavior.
In order to accomplish this I have offered a series of
hypotheses (albeit incomplete) through which the
theory can be tested. While these hypotheses are
framed within the discipline of medical anthropology
it is my hope that they can be extended to other
lines of research.

BIBLIOGRAPHY

Ackerknecht, E. (1965). *History and geography of the world's most important diseases.* New York and London, Hafner.

Alland, Alexander, Jr. (1966). Medical anthropology and the study of biological and cultural adaptation. *American Anthropologist* 68:40-51.

——— (1967). *Evolution and human behavior.* New York, Natural History Press.

Angel, J. L. (1966). Porotic hyperostosis, anemias, malarias, and marshes in the prehistoric Eastern Mediterranean. *Science* 153:760-63.

Baker, P. T. (1963). Adaptation to high altitude cold in the Andes Annual Progress Report. 1 July, Contract No. Da-49-193-MD-2260, Office of the Surgeon General.

Baker, P. T., and J. Weiner (1966). *The biology of human adaptability.* Oxford, Clarendon Press.

Balicki, A. (1963). Shamanistic behavior among the Netsilik Eskimo. *Southwestern Journal of Anthropology* 19: 380-91.

Bates, M. (1949). *The natural history of mosquitoes.* New York, Harper Torchbooks.

Blumberg, B. S., ed. (1962). Proceedings of the conference on genetic polymorphisms and geographic variations in disease. New York, Grune and Stratton.

BIBLIOGRAPHY

Bowen, E. (1954). *Return to laughter.* London, Victor Gollanez.

Brace, C. L., and A. Montagu (1966). *Man's evolution.* New York, Macmillan.

Brothwell, D. R. (1963). *Digging up bones.* London, British Museum.

Buettner-Janusch, J. (1958). Natural selection in man: the ABO(H) blood group system. *American Anthropologist* 60:437-56.

Burnett, M. F. (1966). *Natural history of infectious disease.* New York, Cambridge University Press.

Burrows, W. (1954). *Textbook of microbiology,* 16th edition. Philadelphia, W. B. Saunders.

Campbell, D. T. (1965). Variation and retention in sociocultural evolution. In *Social change in developing areas,* edited by R. Barringer, G. I. Blanksten, and R. W. Mack. Cambridge, Mass., Shenkman 19-47.

Childe, V. G. (1936). *Man makes himself.* London, C. A. Watts and Co.

―――― (1951). *Social evolution.* New York, Henry Schuman.

Collins, P. (1965). Functional analysis in the symposium Man, culture, and animals. In *Man, culture, and animals,* Publication No. 78 of the American Association for the Advancement of Science, Washington, D.C., 271-82.

Cravioto, J., E. R. Delicardie, and H. G. Birch (1966). Nutrition, growth and neurointegrative development: an experiment and ecological study. *Pediatrics 38,* No. 2, Part II, 319-72.

Currier, R. L. (1966). The hot cold syndrome and symbolic balance in Mexican and Spanish-American folk medicine. *Ethnology* V:251-63.

Davenport, W. (1960). Jamaican fishing: a game theory analysis. Yale University Publications in *Anthropology* No. 59.

Dobzhansky, T. (1962). *Mankind evolving.* New Haven, Yale University Press.

Dubos, R. (1965). *Man adapting.* New Haven, Yale University Press.

Dunn, F. (1965). On the antiquity of malaria in the Western Hemisphere. *Human Biology* 37:385-93.

Eggan, F. (1954). Social anthropology and the method of controlled comparison. *American Anthropologist* 56: 743-63.

———— (1966). *The American Indian.* Chicago, Aldine Press.

Evans-Pritchard, E. E. (1937). *Witchcraft oracles and magic among the Azande.* New York, Oxford University Press.

Field, M. (1937). *Religion and medicine of the Gà people.* New York, Oxford University Press.

Fortune, R. (1963). *Sorcerers of Dobu.* New York, E. P. Dutton.

Fox, R., and L. Tiger (1966). The zoological perspective in social science. *Man,* new series, 1:75-81.

Gadjusek, C. (1964). Factors governing the genetics of primitive human populations. *Cold Spring Harbor symposia on quantitative biology,* Vol. XXIX:121-36.

Geertz, C. (1962). The growth of culture and the evolution of mind. *Theories of the mind,* Jordan Scher, ed. Glencoe, Free Press.

Gelfand, M. (1965). *Witch doctor.* New York, Praeger.

Githens, T. S. (1948). Drug plants of Africa. *African Handbooks* No. 8. Philadelphia, University of Pennsylvania Press.

Goffman, E. (1959). *The presentation of self in everyday life.* New York, Anchor Books.

Goodman, M. (1963). Man's place in the phyllogeny of the primates as reflected in serum proteins. In *Classification and human evolution,* edited by Sherwood Washborn. Chicago, Aldine Press. 204-34.

Gorman, J. G. (1964). Selection against the Rh-negative gene by malaria. *Nature,* 202, 4933:676-77.

Hallowell, A. I. (1955). *Culture and experience.* Philadelphia, University of Pennsylvania Press.

Harley, G. W. (1941). *Native African medicine.* Cambridge, Harvard Press.

Hempel, C. (1959). The logic of functional analysis. *Sym-*

posium on sociological theory, Llewellyn Gross, ed. Evanston, Ill., Row Peterson. 271-307.

Huxley, J. (1943). *Evolution the modern synthesis.* New York, Harper & Bros.

Huxley, J., E. Mayr, H. Osmond, and A. Hoffer (1964). Schizophrenia as a genetic morphism. *Nature* 204:220-21.

Jarco, S. (1966). *Human paleopathology.* New Haven, Yale University Press.

Kardiner, A. (1939). *The individual and his society.* New York, Columbia University Press.

Kerharo, J., and Bouquet, A. (1950). *Plantes medicinales et toxique en la Cote d'Ivoire et Haute-Volta.* Paris, Vigot Freres.

Kluckhohn, C. (1944). *Navaho witchcraft.* Cambridge, Beacon Press.

Kroeber, A. L. (1952). The superorganic. *The nature of culture,* by A. L. Kroeber. Chicago, University of Chicago Press. 22-51.

Kunstadter, P., R. Buhler, F. F. Stephan, C. F. Westoff (1963). Demographic variability and preferential marriage patterns. *American Journal of Physical Anthropology* 21: 511-19.

Laughlin, W. (1962). *Primitive theory of medicine: empirical knowledge.* Conference on Medicine and Anthropology, Arden House, Harriman, N. Y. Nov. 17-20 1961.

Levi-Strauss, C. (1949). *Les structures elementaires de la parenté.* Paris.

Livingstone, F. (1958). Anthropological implications of sickle cell gene in west Africa. *American Anthropologist* 60:533-62.

May, J. (1958). *The ecology of infectious disease,* Vol. I. New York Geographical Society.

Moore, O. K. (1957). Divination, a new perspective. *American Anthropologist* 59:69-74.

Morgan, L. H. (1877). *Ancient society.* New York, Holt.

Mozley, A. (1953). *A Background for the prevention of bilhirza.* London, H. K. Lewis.

Murdock, G. P. (1949). *Social structure.* New York, Macmillan.

———— (1955). North American social organization. *Davidson Journal of Anthropology* 1:85-97.

———— (1959a). *Africa.* New York, McGraw-Hill.

———— (1959b). Evolution in social organization. *Evolution and Anthropology*, edited by B. Meggers. Anthropological Society of Washington. 126-45.

Nagel, E. (1961). *The structure of science.* New York, Harcourt, Brace.

Needham, R. (1960). *Structure and sentiment.* Chicago, University of Chicago Press.

Nurge, E. (1958). Etiology of illness in Guinhangdan. *American Anthropologist* 60:1158-72.

Osgood, C. (1959). *Ingalik mental culture.* New Haven, Yale University Publications in Anthropology, 56.

Otten, C. (1967). On pestilence, diet, natural selection, and the distribution of microbial and human blood group antigens and antibodies. *Current Anthropology* 8:209-27.

Park, M. (1801). *Travels and recent discoveries in Africa in the Years 1796 and 1797.* New York, McFarlane for Alexander Brodie.

Radcliffe-Brown, A. R. N. (1952). *Structure and function in primitive society.* Glencoe, The Free Press.

Rappaport, R. (1968). *Pigs for the ancestors.* Yale University Press.

Riesenberg, S. (1948). Magic and medicine in Ponape. *Southwestern Journal of Anthropology* 4:406-29.

Rivers, W. H. (1914). *Kinship and social organization.* London, Constable and Co., Ltd.

Roberts, R. S. (1966). The place of plague in English history. *Royal Society of Medicine Proceedings* 59:101-05.

Rosman, A. (1962). Social structure and acculturation among the Kanuri of Northern Nigeria. Ann Arbor, University Microfilms.

Sahlins, M. (1968). Notes on the original affluent society in *Man the Hunter*, edited by Richard Lee and Irven DeVore, Chicago, Aldine Press.

Sahlins, M., and E. Service (1960). *Evolution and culture.* Ann Arbor, University of Michigan Press.

193

BIBLIOGRAPHY

Scrimshaw, N. (1963). Factors influencing protein requirements. *The Harvey Lectures Series* 58:181-216.

Selye, H. (1956). *The stress of life.* New York, McGraw-Hill.

Simpson, G. G. (1961). Comments on cultural evolution. *Daedalus* 90:514-18.

Spencer, H. (1864). *First principles.* New York, Appleton.

Steward, J. (1937). Ecological Aspects of Southwestern society. *Anthropos* 32:87-104.

———— (1958). *Theory of culture change.* Urbana, University of Illinois Press.

Thiessen, D. D. (1964). Population density and behavior: A review of theoretical and physiological contributions. *Texas Reports on Biology and Medicine 22, No. 2,* 266-314.

Tylor, E. B. (1871). *Primitive culture.* London, John Murray.

Vavilov, N. I. (1951). *The origin, variation, immunity and breeding of cultivated plants.* New York, Ronald Press.

Vayda, A. P., and R. A. Rappaport (1968). Ecology: cultural and non-cultural. *Introduction to cultural anthropology,* edited by James Clifton. Boston, Houghton Mifflin.

Wallace, A. F. C. (1961). *Culture and personality.* New York, Random House.

Washburn, S. (1959). Speculations on the interrelations of the history of tools and biological evolution. *The evolution of man's capacity for culture,* by Spuhler. Detroit, Wayne State University Press.

Weisenfeld, S. L. (1967). Sickle cell trait in human biological and cultural evolution. *Science* 157:1134-40.

White, L. (1959). *The evolution of culture.* New York, McGraw-Hill.

Whiting, J. (1964). Effects of climate on certain cultural practices. *Explorations in cultural anthropology,* edited by Ward H. Goodenough. New York, McGraw-Hill. 511-4.

————, **and I. Child** (1953). *Child training and personality.* New Haven, Yale University Press.

Williams, G. (1966). *Adaptation and natural selection.* Princeton, N.J., Princeton University Press.

INDEX

Abortions, 71 f.
Abron (West Africa), 115, 141
  attitude to Western medi-
    cine, 170
  effects of Western medicine
    on, 158-78
  medical categories of,
    136 ff., 139, 163
  medications of, 120, 122, 125
  sacrifices to dead, 142
  witches and sorcerers, 145
Accommodation, between
    host and organism, 94 ff.,
    98 f.
Acculturation, Ch. 7
Ackerknecht, E., 28
Adaptation, 179 ff.
  internal and external, 40 ff.,
    45 f.
  measurement of, 31, 36 ff.,
    42, 180 f.
  to disease, Ch. 4
Adaptive fit, 31, 35, 41
Africa (Murdock), 38
Alchemist, The (Jonson), 54 f.
Alkaloids, as medication, 119
American Indian, The
    (Eggan), 38
Amino acids, 68 f., 71
  resistance-building and, 76
Anaerobic organisms, 21, 58
Ancestors, in disease etiology,
    142 ff.
Angel, J. L., 98
Anthraquinone cathartics, 120

Antibiotics, 171
Antihelminthic glucosides,
    119
Antisera, *see* Serums
Anxiety, 82, 135
Archaeology, 42, 96-98
Arthritis, 19, 97
Arthropods, 23, 28
"Avoidance therapies," 123-24
Aymara Indians (Bolivia), 121

Bacilli, 25
Bacteria, types of, 25 f.
Baker, P. T., 83
Balicki, A., 142, 145, 150 f.
Bates, M., 60 f.
Bemba (East Africa), 75
Bick, Georgeda, 75
Birth rate, 22
Blood, studies of, 13 f.
Blood groups, and resistance
    to disease, 102-107
Body size, and nutrition, 75
Bone, *see* Skeletal material
Bouquet, A., 163
Bowen, E., 153
Brace, C. L., 33
Brothwell, D. R., 97
Buettner-Janusch, J., 104
Burnett, M. F., 98
Burrows, W., 101

Caloric requirements, 70, 77 f.
Campbell, D. T., 31
Cancer, 24

INDEX

INDEX

Environmental determinism, 34 f., 39
Enzootic disease, 20
Epidemic disease, 20, 52 ff., 91
  cyclical, 64
  dispersal and, 153 f.
Epizootic disease, 20
Erythroblastosis, 106 f.
Eskimos, 78, 94
Essential oils, as medication, 119-20
Ethnomedical theory, *see* Ethnoscience; Medicine, non-Western
Ethnoscience, 9 ff., 89, 93, 129
  as reinforcement, 7
  see also Medicine, non-Western
European folk-medicine, 126
Evans-Pritchard, E. E., 145
Evolution, "anti-entropic" theory of, 33
  biological theory of, 5 f., Ch. 2
  cultural, 86-89, 179 ff.
  game theory and, 86 f.
  indeterminacy in, 39
  nonlinear theories of, 32 f.
  parallel, 42
  of primates, 40
  "specific," 33
  unilineal theories of, 32 f.
Evolutionary potential, law of, 31
Evolutionism, in social anthropology, 5, Ch. 2
Experimentation, 9
External adaptation, 40 ff., 46, 49, 186
Extinction, 36, 38, 87
  of culture traits, 44
  of parasites, 99

Fats, as medication, 118
Feces, human, use as fertilizer, 13, 56, 95, 131 f.
  as medication, 126
  storage of, 131 f.
Fecundity, 22
Feedbacks, between behavior and disease, 67, 94 f., 130 f.
  between behavior and environment, 5, 49, 186
  between behavior and genetic change, 50 f.
  physical disorders and, 8
  positive, 183 f., 186
  psychosomatic disorders and, 8
Fertility, 22, 42, 45
  as measure of adaptation, 42, 86 f.
  crowding and, 84
  post partum taboos and, 141 f.
  witchcraft and, 146
Fertilization, by human feces, 13, 56, 95, 131 f.
Flat worms, 27
Flexibility, in population strategies, 4, 87
Folk medicine, *see* Medicine, non-Western
Folk models, 9 f.; *see also* Ethnoscience
  development of, 18
Fortune, R., 143
"Founder effect," 107
Fox, R., 32
Functional analysis, 41 f., 183 f.
Functional disorders, 19
Functional systems, *see* Homeostasis

INDEX

INDEX